YOUR TOWNS & CITIES IN

SUSSEX

AT WAR 1939–45

Sources

Battle Over Sussex 1940 Pat Burgess & Andy Saunders, Middleton Press 1990

Bexhill Observer

Bexhill Public Library

Blitz Over Sussex 1941–42 Pat Burgess & Andy Saunders, Middleton Press 1994

Bognor Regis Observer (BX OBS)

Bognor Regis Public Library

Bombers Over Sussex 1943–45 Pat Burgess & Andy Saunders, Middleton Press 1995

Brighton Gazette

Chichester Observer (CHI OBS)

D Day West Sussex Ian Greig, Kim Leslie & Alan Readman

Eastbourne Public Library

Frontline Sussex Martin Mace

Hastings Public Library

Hastings In Peace & War Mary Haskell Porter

Hastings & St Leonards Observer (HS&STL OBS)

Kent & Sussex 1940 Stuart Hylton

Kent & Sussex Gazette (K&SX G)

Littlehampton Observer (L OBS)

Littlehampton Through the Wars H.J.F.

Mid Sussex Express (MSX)

Portsmouth Evening News (PEN)

RAF Tangmere Revisited

Rye Public Library

Secret Sussex Resistance Stewart Angel

Shoreham Herald (SH)

Sussex Airfields in the Second World War J. Brooks

Sussex Advertiser (SA)

Sussex Express (SX EXP)

Sussex Home Guard Paul Crook

Sussex Wartime Relics & Memorials 1939–1945 Martin Mace

The British Newspaper Archive

The Military Defence Of West Sussex John Goodwin

Wartime Littlehampton Iris Jones

West Sussex Gazette (WSG)

West Sussex Records Office (WSRO)

Worthing At War Colin Clark & Rupert Taylor

Worthing Public Library

YOUR TOWNS & CITIES IN WORLD WAR TWO

SUSSEX

AT WAR 1939–45

CLIFFORD MEWETT

Pen & Sword
MILITARY

First published in Great Britain in 2018 by
Pen & Sword Military
An imprint of
Pen & Sword Books Ltd
Yorkshire – Philadelphia

ISBN 978 1 47385 559 5

A CIP catalogue record for this book is
available from the British Library.

Printed and bound in England
By CPI Group (UK) Ltd, Croydon, CR0 4YY
Typeset by Aura Technology and Software Services, India

Pen & Sword Books Limited incorporates the imprints of Atlas, Archaeology,
Aviation, Discovery, Family History, Fiction, History, Maritime, Military, Military
Classics, Politics, Select, Transport, True Crime, Air World, Frontline Publishing,
Leo Cooper, Remember When, Seaforth Publishing, The Praetorian Press,
Wharncliffe Local History, Wharncliffe Transport, Wharncliffe True Crime and
White Owl.

For a complete list of Pen & Sword titles please contact

PEN & SWORD BOOKS LIMITED
47 Church Street, Barnsley, South Yorkshire, S70 2AS, England
E-mail: enquiries@pen-and-sword.co.uk
Website: www.pen-and-sword.co.uk

Or
PEN AND SWORD BOOKS
1950 Lawrence Rd, Havertown, PA 19083, USA
E-mail: Uspen-and-sword@casematepublishers.com
Website: www.penandswordbooks.com

Contents

Friends or foes

With the Great War twenty years in the past, relationships between Great Britain and Germany were deteriorating once more. However, this did not deter ordinary citizens of both countries forming their own friendships when two groups of Germans visited Sussex, each on exchange visits, receiving contrasting welcomes.

The first, which proved to be controversial, was a German police football team, paying a return visit to Brighton. Earlier in the year, members of the Brighton and Hove police forces, including the two Chief Constables, had made a trip to Germany, where they were lavishly entertained and played some keenly contested football matches against the Nazi police teams. Now they were reciprocating:

> The party arrived at Hove Station on Sunday evening, to be warmly greeted by the majority of the large crowd that had assembled and anything but cordially by an insignificant minority. Long before the London train arrived it was evident that trouble was anticipated and the police of both local forces, who came to welcome their guests, were also preparing to deal with any emergency. Among the crowd were agitators, some carrying crudely scrawled posters in English and German, bearing such inscriptions as: "we do not want Fascism here", while long haired youths offered for sale copies of a certain paper with extreme views and a van equipped with loud speakers which had been engaged by the Communists, took up a position opposite the station entrance. The atmosphere was tense. The Salvation Army Band then arrived on the scene and were escorted to the Station Approach.
>
> Councillor HC Andrews, of Hove, founder-organiser of the Anglo-German Fellowship League and representatives of the local police forces received the visitors as they alighted and conducted them by way of the luggage entrance to the covered carriageway on the south side of the station, where their appearance was the signal for an outburst of cheering, mingled with boos and shouts of derision. It was evident that the visitors and their hosts were all feeling a trifle uncomfortable. Then, with the former lined up, with the

Chief Constables of Brighton and Hove, both in uniform and other Officers in and out of uniform facing them at attention, the band played the German National Anthem, while the visitors extended their hands in the Nazi Salute. Simultaneously the agitators bellowed the "Internationale" and raised their clenched fists and in the pause that followed, various shouts were drowned by renewed cheers and applause, as uniformed policemen surrounded the agitators and quietly but forcibly removed them from the immediate neighbourhood of the parade. But it was noticeable that during the playing of our own National Anthem perfect quiet reigned and that there were few men in the crowd who did not bare their heads. Then, as the Salvation Army Band marched off a Communist placard was thrust high above the crowd, only to be snatched down by Police Officers and thereafter peace reigned. *(WSG)*

By contrast, at about the same time, a group of German ex-servicemen were enjoying a visit to Sussex as guests of the Horsham Branch of the British Legion, supported by the legion branches of Chichester, Brighton, Arundel, Petworth and Billingshurst. They too were on a return visit, where they were received 'with typical British hospitality'.

After spending their last day in Horsham, the German party were entertained to a farewell dinner at the Black Horse Hotel, 'where they had been so well looked after throughout their stay.'

At the dinner, their leader Baron von Lersner said:

We have been entertained by members of the British Legion, not only as guests, but as real friends and I believe that more and more of these exchange visits of ex-Service men are far the best way of mutual understanding between the peoples, because ex-Service men are always open minded towards each other and they say the truth and that is what we want and the need for real peace. Twenty years ago we were all in the trenches. Today let us build new trenches of friendship and for the joy of our two peoples to come together. As a sign of that spirit with which we are going back to Germany to speak of our English friends, we would like the Horsham Branch to accept a swastika emblem in memory of our stay. If you would put it on your Standard we shall be very much honoured. *(WSG)*

Responding, Lieutenant-Colonel Bowater-Vernon said: 'I do believe we are beginning to realise it is worthwhile to work for peace. I am going away feeling that I have made fifteen good friends.'

The scenes the following day at Horsham Station were remarkable as the Germans left:

After exhausting the supply of platform tickets, several hundred people attended Horsham Station, singing popular songs to the accompaniment of piano accordions. This was the scene which marked the departure of the party of German ex-service men, at the end of their weeks stay. They had been welcomed everywhere with the same kindness accorded to the Horsham Legionnaires when they visited Germany last year. It was an amazing scene at Horsham Station, when British and German comrades and a large gathering of local folk joined in singing each other's National Anthems, "The More We Are Together" and "Auld Lang Syne", culminating in exchanges of "Goot-bye" and "Auf Wiedersehn". *(WSG)*

Their visit had been a tremendous success. However, in less than twelve months, both countries would again be at war.

CHAPTER 1

Recruitment

War seemed likely following the German Fuehrer Adolf Hitler's expansionist policies of re-armament and the re-militarisation of the Rhineland in 1936. Then the occupation of Austria in the spring of 1938 caused considerable alarm throughout Europe. Further expansion aimed at occupying the Sudentenland, a German speaking country that had been under Czech control since the end of the Great War, led to a summit meeting in Munich on 29 September 1938 between Britain, France, Italy and Germany. This resulted in an agreement that the Sudentenland be transferred to Germany in exchange for 'peace in our time'. Great Britain breathed a sigh of relief, but war seemed inevitable and preparations had to be made for it.

In the late 1930s, there were considerable concerns regarding the strength of the two Royal Sussex Regiment Territorial Battalions: the 4th being in West Sussex and the 5th in the east of the county. Concern was expressed by the *West Sussex Gazette* in January 1938 that the strength of the 4th Battalion had only increased by forty-seven during 1937, 'notwithstanding the publicity given to the need for more men and the efforts of a few keen residents who have done their best to get other recruiters to work in the interests of the Battalion.' Their correspondent, in his opinion, blamed 'slackness, incompetence and a lack of practical patriotism'.

With the blessing of the War Office, the Sussex Territorial Army Association set out to recruit a further 720 men through its local recruiting committees.

There were valid reasons as to why recruitment was slow. Among the concerns for prospective recruits was the time they would have to take off from work to attend drills and camps. Would their employers release them? And how would it affect their incomes? Would their pay continue or stop during periods of training? Would the annual camps affect their normal holiday entitlements? Travelling to attend parades was also a consideration, especially in rural areas that recruited men from the many outlying villages and hamlets.

The recruiting committees worked with local Commanding Officers and employers alike, who were encouraged to perform their patriotic duty by releasing their men. This was particularly difficult when there were only two or three men on the staff. They also encouraged local residents to take an interest in the welfare of units raised in their midst, especially in rural districts. Local village football and cricket clubs were also approached. Pulborough did particularly well; it was a large area recruiting men from eleven outlying parishes and with the help of the Sussex army recruiting staff, put on a successful recruiting evening where, among other items, visitors were shown the new anti-tank rifles and Bren guns. Recruiting literature was also distributed.

Recruiting parades became a feature in Sussex. One in Worthing took the form of a march from the town centre to Broadwater Green, where a demonstration of some light tanks from Farnborough attracted 'much attention', as did the sixteen rounds fired by the Royal Artillery, with the infantry giving a demonstration in putting up a smoke screen. During the evening a flight of Hawker Hurricane fighters from RAF Tangmere flew in formation over the seafront. The day proved to be successful, the recruiting office in the old Town Hall reported a steady flow of applicants.

A large crowd attended the opening of a recruitment week in Bognor Regis, entertained at the beginning by a loudspeaker van playing popular marches, culminating in Sussex by the Sea. Displays by the Royal Sussex Regiment and an RAF team were supported by the local fire brigade. An appeal for young men to join-up was made by Brigadier-General W.L. Osborn, the Colonel of the Royal Sussex Regiment, who informed the meeting that the Bognor drill hall in Bedford Street would be open all week and thereafter two nights a week between 6pm and 8.30pm:

> If Bognor recruits are so badly needed, the Recruiting Office should be open every day all day long and not simply for two or three hours on two evenings a week! *(WSG)*

The Munich Crisis and the formation of new units in Sussex led to more urgent recruiting. This strong campaign continued into 1939 and was a success, confirmed in April when the War Office sent a telegram to the Commanding Officer of the 4th Battalion, congratulating him on reaching war establishment:

> Sussex has been responding well to the urgent call for more Territorials. Not long ago we had to draw attention to the fact that the Battalion was seriously short of men and we did this repeatedly because too many people failed to realise that the international situation was likely to get worse and that the delay in raising recruits was dangerous. *(WSG)*

The position of the 5th Battalion was also below strength. Rotary Clubs were targeted by the War Office to boost recruiting. Eastbourne was particularly bad:

> The country would be in a parlous state if the numbers of Territorials in the rest of Sussex were as low a percentage of the population as that of Eastbourne, there is a feeling that we can leave it all to the Navy to stop any invasion. *(SX EXP)*

Steadily the situation improved, with between forty and fifty recruits a day being processed by the Territorial Office in North Street, Brighton:

> On Thursday morning a boy of fifteen presented himself at the Recruiting Office, eager to become a bugler in "The Fifth" and was delighted when told that, subject to the consent of his parents he would be duly enlisted. *(WSG)*

Other Sussex Territorial units, the seven batteries of the Royal Artillery and their two signal sections were up to strength, as were the Anti-Aircraft Searchlight Unit and the Royal Army Service Corps.

Throughout Sussex, new drill halls were built, the two largest being the headquarters of the 70th (Sussex) Searchlight Regiment in Dyke Road, Brighton, and the Worthing drill hall situated on the A27. Others were planned for Pulborough, Arundel, Steyning and Hailsham, whilst many of the existing drill halls were renovated.

In July 1939, the Field Force units of the Sussex Territorial Army Association were reported as being completed to War Establishment and were mobilised on 6 September.

Women were also to play their part in the Army, when the Government introduced the Women's Auxiliary Territorial Service (ATS) in September 1938. This embodied the Women's Transport Service (FANY), a Volunteer Transport Corps and the Women's Legion. The ATS were attached to the Territorial Army, the women serving receiving two-thirds of the pay of the male soldiers.

The Royal Naval Wireless Auxiliary Reserve was a specialist organisation trained in naval procedure for service at home or abroad, ashore or afloat, in time of war. Its recruitment was aimed particularly at men who held the Postmaster General's certificates and other radio enthusiasts who were interested in the transmission of wireless messages. This particular section was based in Brighton and, apart from the above requirements, prospective recruits had to have been born of British parents, be between the ages of 18 and 55, with no ties that would prevent them joining the Royal Navy in the time of war. Applicants also needed a knowledge of Morse Code and either be in possession of, or able to construct, a high frequency radio receiver.

The Royal Air Force were also recruiting, 'to meet increased requirements' targeting boys of school certificate or approximately equivalent educational standard.

The well-known aviator Sir Alan Cobham was himself 'recruited' to speak to the audience at the Odeon Cinema, Chichester, regarding the opportunities available to young men joining the Royal Air Force:

I thought there would be a long waiting list for entry into the Royal Air Force, but there is not a waiting list and I am astounded. For young men can prepare for the best of jobs while serving in the Air Force. The RAF provided a fine career for young men and a good opportunity when they left the service. Any engineer coming out of the RAF could get a job immediately and there were also opportunities for other craftsman. In fact no finer service existed, for it provided such a variety of occupation and life. Enthusiasts in wireless, photography, woodwork and flying work were all provided for and flying was not difficult to learn, anyone with normal intelligence could pick it up, or else half of my friends would not be flying! The young men who joined the RAF were on a good thing. *(WSG)*

His appeal was backed up by a display in the foyer of RAF equipment and photographs of aeroplanes in use at the Ford Naval School, under the supervision of serving RAF personnel.

During their work up to the war, the RAF lost aircraft over Sussex.

One of twelve bombers arriving at RAF Thorney Island, at night, ran out of fuel whilst completing an extra circuit to allow another aircraft in difficulties to land first. The doomed aircraft nose-dived into the mud of Prinsted Channel having avoided the village in the dark conditions. The crew of two survived.

The same week another crashed on the East Sussex village of Udimore, whilst engaged in night observation work. With only one engine working and the other threatening to fail, the pilot headed back to land and ordered the crew to bail-out, they all landed safely between Udimore and Brede. The aircraft crashed in Park Wood nearby.

The next accident was more tragic when a single-seat fighter based at the Reserve Flying School at Gatwick lost power over Brighton and crashed in

Sir Alan Cobham and his RAF recruiters (West Sussex Gazette)

Freshfield Road, destroying a house in which a young housewife was preparing a meal, and killing her two daughters, both under 5, who were playing in the garden. The pilot was also killed.

Further crashes involved an Anson on a reconnaissance flight that came to grief at the top of Kingston Hill near Lewes in foggy conditions, and a Gloster Gladiator based at RAF Kenley also became a fog victim. On another hill at Alciston, a single-seat fighter was lost when it destroyed a house at Crowborough, killing the pilot and a lady in service.

In August the militiamen received their orders. These were members of an elite unit consisting of single men only, which came into being after the Munich Agreement. Open to men between the ages of 20 until the day before their 22nd birthdays, militiamen completed a six months full-time training course before returning to civilian life, where for approximately one year they were subject to immediate call-up. When their individual year was up, they then joined the normal reserve units. With the outbreak of war they gradually lost their identity. However, that was after the first militiamen throughout Sussex were called-up:

> The first detachment of Worthing's militiamen has left to join their units. To some the break with home ties or the temporary relinquishment of a career on which they have just embarked will entail some hardship. In compensation they will have the opportunity of attaining a physical fitness which probably they would not otherwise have acquired, coupled with the knowledge that they are fitting themselves to play a full part in the defence of their Country.

Army recruits under the watchful eye of a sergeant going to lunch (West Sussex Library Service PP-WSL-FLA-PO156)

We believe that it is in this spirit that the great majority willingly undertake this service. They are carrying out a national duty in its highest form, that of personal service. *(WSG)*

At the end of September 1939, a proclamation was made by the king directing that, with certain exemptions, all male British subjects who were wthin Great Britain on 1 October and who at that date had attained the age of 20, but had not attained the age of 22, were liable for service in the armed forces of the Crown and were instructed to register at their local Ministry of Labour and National Service Office. Any British subjects of these ages who were outside Great Britain on 1 October were liable to be called-up for service as soon as they returned to the United Kingdom.

CHAPTER 2

Sussex prepares

Throughout Sussex in towns and villages as the prospect of war became increasingly evident, people were stepping forward to 'do their bit' in a variety of organisations.

Perhaps one of the most well-known wartime organisations was the Women's Land Army, which was re-founded in June 1939 as the prospect of war became imminent. These were girls trained to replace the farm workers who would

Land army girls harvesting peas at Brinsbury Farm, Pulborough (Garland Collection N51482)

be called-up if war was declared, thus maintaining food supplies. There were estimated to be hundreds of farmers in Sussex who would benefit from this movement, but initial interest was slow and patchy.

Recruiting commenced immediately with a county office opened in Horsham where the women were accepted between the ages of 18 to 53. The Ministry of Agriculture and Fisheries provided training courses from July in general farming, tractor-driving, poultry work, forestry, market gardening, fruit-farming and dairy work, including the skill of how to milk a cow. These took place at the School of Agriculture at Plumpton, whilst local education authorities and individual farmers also assisted and were paid 15s (75p) a week as a board and allowance for the girls if they undertook to give them four weeks training in general farm-work:

> In various parts of Sussex, members of the Women's Land Army, grouped in ones and twos on various farms, are receiving a month's basic training to enable them to replace those agricultural workers who at intervals may be called up into the armed forces. *(SX EXP)*

Land Army girls were provided with a complete working outfit of breeches, pullover, mackintosh, dungarees, stockings, hat and an overall coat. As well as the free uniforms the women worked for 28 shillings a week initially, although their pay did increase later in the war, out of which they had to pay their board and lodging (but only during the four weeks training at the School of Agriculture). The women worked a six-and-a-half-day week and had a three-day paid holiday entitlement when they had been employed by the same farmer for six months, with a further two days after another six months.

To boost numbers an urgent appeal was launched county wide for more girls to form an auxiliary force. Here girls could give four weeks short term seasonal work as required.

The writer Sheila Kaye-Smith in an article in the *Bexhill Observer* wrote:

> The woman who joins the Land Army is not joining a merely Auxiliary Service. She is stepping into the very first line of home defence and taking her place shoulder to shoulder with the men who have undertaken the vital work of feeding this Country in time of war. Farming may not seem an adventurous occupation, but it is none the less a job for the adventurous. Those women who would like to join the Land Army but have ties which prevent their taking on full-time service, can be enrolled in the Auxiliary Force for harvest work only, a minimum period of four weeks. A shortage of farm workers corresponds this year with a large increase in cultivation

as thousands of new acres have been put under the plough. That these crops should be gathered in and the work on farms not only maintained but greatly enlarged, is a work of national importance, which should stand second to none in its appeal to women and girls. *(BX OBS)*

Miss Mildred Wingham from Chichester was the first girl from Sussex to become a fully qualified trainee. Writing home, she described her experiences attempting to milk a cow:

Well do I remember that first morning! I found myself in a cowshed at some very early hour, clad in a white smock and seated on a low stool near the hindermost end of a cow, a pail between my knees. The farm bailiff was trying to instil into my unresponsive brain some knowledge of the gentle art of milking. Having given me a practical demonstration, he left me to work things out for myself.

My progress was very slow. All I could produce was a minute, uncertain trickle. My arms ached and my spirits drooped, though the latter revived temporarily on the rare occasions when I managed to produce a few good, full-bodied squirts. I watched enviously while the cowman worked, the milk sang into his bucket, first with a high-pitched note, changing to a deep, rhythmic "zug-zug" as the white foam danced to the brim.

Wondering, not very hopefully, whether I should ever be able to make it perform in like fashion, I turned to extracting pathetic drips from Kingcup, a long suffering animal, who regarded me wearily. She is our "beginners cow", comparatively easy to milk and unable to kick, having broken her leg in infancy. We were both relieved when the bailiff arrived and deciding that Kingcup had put up with enough for one day, quickly finished the job for me.

During the next few days I improved a little and graduated to Columbine, a pretty Jersey. Following instructions, I bribed her with a bowl of cake and sat down hopefully and for about a minute all went well. Then the stream began to fade and soon petered out.

"Come on old girl, be helpful!" Columbine, her silvery nose buried in the manger, her prehensile tongue reaching after straying pieces of cake, was apathetic, so I sought advice from those who knew.

"Keep on stripping and she will let the milk down", I was told and sure enough after five minutes of this treatment, combined with alternate threats and pleading, she did! But she consented to give me only sixteen pounds of her usual twenty and it was some days before she would allow me to take all her milk. *(WSG)*

Mildred Wingham at work, milking (West Sussex Gazette)

As the days passed the aching in my arms grew less. I gradually increased my speed and was able to milk a greater number of cows. I began then to take a genuine pleasure in milking, which seemed so easy that I could not understand why I ever found it so difficult. I have now forsaken the gentle Kingcup and her kind hearted colleagues for some of the more restive animals. I shut my eyes while they execute high kicks, which are worthy of chorus girls, in the vicinity of the bucket, but I have not yet lost any of its precious contents. (WSG)

At its peak, more than 3,700 Land Army girls volunteered to serve in Sussex and were regularly visited by their county representatives, who did a lot to ensure that the girls were accepted into the social life of the villages where they were employed.

Red Cross detachments were started throughout the county. A detachment consisted of twelve people and a commandant, whose members worked in hospitals and convalescent homes providing nursing services for the sick and wounded. Private properties were also commandeered to house patients. An appeal went out in 1938 calling for volunteer motor car drivers:

> In a national emergency, the British Red Cross will be called upon to supply motor car drivers for the large number of improvised ambulances which will be needed over and above the ambulances already possessed by municipalities, police and the voluntary services. Should air raids occur, the demands for ambulance transport will be far in excess of any peacetime requirement; mobility in handling air raid casualties is an essential part of first aid to the injured.
>
> Volunteers to drive such improvised ambulances are required for this service. There are no obligations or duties in times of peace. Experienced drivers of both sexes are wanted and men should be over thirty. Will ladies and gentlemen in Sussex who are willing to be registered for this service kindly send their names to the address given. *(WSG)*.

The Petworth Red Cross detachment being inspected by the Duchess of Norfolk in 1941 (Garland Collection N20560)

The following words were spoken by Lieutenant-Colonel H.I. Powell-Edwards, at a gathering in Ditchling, East Sussex, to create interest in forming a local detachment of the Red Cross:

> In Britain things could be done better under a voluntary system than they were in some Countries under compulsion. The strength of the voluntary system was in the fact that people who worked under it were governed by love of Country and the work they selected to do. The Country would never have the chance, as in the past, of turning round to get ready for war and it was necessary, therefore, for people to be trained and ready to meet all emergencies.

When war was declared, they and the Order of St John's joined forces, becoming the joint war organisation under the Red Cross emblem, expanding their roles to the sending of food parcels, books and recreational material to our prisoners-of-war.

The Women's Voluntary Service (WVS), was formed in 1938 and could turn their hands to most things, from knitting clothes for servicemen, providing tea and food from emergency canteens and their own vehicles, for fire fighters, helpers and victims following air-raids and supporting those who had lost their homes and

Red Cross nurses training to deal with burns victims (West Sussex Gazette)

possessions. Some who volunteered for car driving had to train to be able to drive at night without lights, as well as being able to change wheels and do small repairs themselves in the case of a breakdown. At Midhurst, Lord Cowdray gave permission for the grounds of Cowdray Park to be used for instruction in convoy driving and night driving without lights.

WVS personnel were also needed for all emergency hospital services, nurses, clerks, ambulance drivers, storekeepers, cleaners, canteen workers and child welfare workers.

One of their first tasks took place around the time of the Munich Crisis when they conducted a county-wide exercise to ascertain how many evacuees Sussex could foster.

An auxiliary force was also recruited, attracting women who could only give a short period of service, school teachers for instance, who volunteered during the summer holidays.

In East Sussex, a section of the Women's Transport Service was already established when a meeting at Faygate, near Horsham, was held to form a West Sussex Section. Those who joined the Transport Service were expected to gain a general knowledge of anti-gas precautions, cookery, catering, convoy work, drill, driving, mechanics, first aid, hygiene, sanitation, map-reading and report-writing. Recruits had to be between 17 and 40 years of age and apart from driving duties, they could be nursing orderlies, cooks, store-keepers, clerks and interpreters. Funded by subscriptions only, members had to provide their own uniforms.

The Sussex County Comforts Association was formed in January 1939 to provide woollen garments, gloves, mittens and mufflers, etc, to the troops. Within a few weeks, 'thousands of Sussex women were knitting busily'. Distribution centres were opened allowing the knitters to concentrate on the work. The wool was supplied at a cheap rate from an official organisation paid for by public subscription.

War preparations became more urgent in September 1938, when the Munich Crisis occurred. Orders were given to issue gas-masks via specially prepared distribution centres. These were generally equipped with a gas-proof room and a mask-room, where the gas-masks were fitted and tested. The masks were fitted with an adjustable strap, which made putting them on a far from pleasant experience. They had a peculiar smell and initially gave the impression of the wearer being suffocated. Small children had 'Mickey Mouse' respirators with two eye pieces, whilst small babies had special carriers in which they could be placed.

In rural areas a gas van visited, where the masks could be tested. At Pulborough the van arrived one Friday evening and, after issuing the gas-masks, the ladies of

Pulborough Red Cross ladies preparing to take the gas-mask test (West Sussex Gazette)

the Pulborough. Detachment of the Red Cross 'went through the van', as did the men of the Midhurst, Petworth and Pulborough Detachments of the 4th Battalion, the Royal Sussex Regiment, (Territorials). This little exercise necessitated the gas-mask being worn and then the person entering the gas filled rear of the van, removing their masks for a few seconds, replacing them and exiting the vehicle – an unpleasant but necessary task.

The Voluntary Aid Detachment was re-formed in 1939, having proved their worth during the Great War, and supported the medical services by providing nurses, as well as pharmacists, radiographers and clerks, among others. Although the VAD was essentially voluntary, it was the object of the organisation that every woman should be registered for some form of service, even if she could only spare an hour or two each week.

An inspection of the VAD in Chester received good reports, with the press concluding:

In the modern form of warfare, with attack from the air coming so much into the picture, the whole of England might someday be in the front line and therefore it was essential that every VAD should be up to scratch, the day would perhaps come when the Country would be grateful to them.

Another exercise took place at Henfield:

Those responsible for the Henfield air raid precautions area have lost no time in putting into practice what they have been trained to do in a state of emergency. Their preparedness was given a very good test at the weekend, when, by arrangement, ARP Headquarters received a report of a supposed air raid on the northernmost part of their area. Warning was received from the warden at Shermanbury that the "raiders" had made a target of Wyemarks, the residence of Colonel AC Watson. All specially trained units, the Fire Brigade, Ambulance Staff, Nursing Detachment, Doctors and Decontamination Squad, the last being fitted with respirators and protective clothing, were rapidly mobilised and conveyed in cars to the scene, where they found the stables and coach house ablaze from an incendiary bomb, a crater and everything smothered with mustard gas. The decontamination squad quickly set to work to remove the gas to enable the others to get busy, whilst firemen put out the flames. Doctors and nurses attended to various appointed casualties and removed them to the house for further treatment and even filling in the craters was not overlooked. *(SX EXP)*

CHAPTER 3

War imminent

Just six years after the end of the Great War, the government of the day created air-raid wardens to advise and protect the population from air attack. Following on from this, in 1937, with an eye on possible future developments, more wardens began to be recruited:

> These Wardens must be reasonably active, though not fit for fire-fighting or other strenuous work; in short, they should be elderly men, not likely to lose their heads if bombs started dropping. *(WSG)*

The Home Office issued a handbook to all local authorities explaining the regulations under which Air-Raid Precaution (ARP) wardens should discharge

Air-raid exercise, Bognor Regis (Frank L'Alouette Collection, by kind permission of Jeanette Hickman)

their statutory duties for the safeguarding of the civilian population, in the event of war breaking out and air-raids occurring. They supplied and gave advice on air-raid shelters to householders, who also received a Home Office handbook, explaining the simple methods of preparing a refuge room, a safe area within their homes, as well as things to do during a war and hints on first aid. Advice was also given on building an emergency trench to accommodate up to six persons. Trenches were also dug in parks and recreation grounds and schools were to be issued with a sufficient quantity of sandbags for their protection.

Slum areas were cleared all over Brighton giving more land for air-raid shelters. With raids anticipated, shelters were built well before the war, constructed very often by local builders. As the war drew nearer, communal shelters were constructed throughout Sussex staffed during air-raids by wardens, after which they had to assess how much emergency and rescue services were required and collate damage reports. For domestic use, Anderson shelters were introduced usually built in gardens, whilst Morrison shelters became widespread for indoors. Wardens were also responsible for enforcing the blackout by patrolling the streets at night to ensure that lights from any building did not show.

An Anderson shelter at Felpham School (Author's collection)

The threat of possible air-raids, including gas attacks, in any future war was very much on the minds of Sussex residents. The *West Sussex Gazette* in January 1938 told the Bognor Regis town councillors to wake their ideas up, commenting on the lack of information the residents had received:

Detailed measures, it is understood, are under consideration, but what these might involve for the ordinary householder remains obscure. The police, under Inspector Dabson and the Red Cross authorities are quietly preparing and the town surely would welcome some sign, such as the calling of joint meetings to co-ordinate organisations and show that the Council, in spite of all delays of which they are not responsible, are tackling in earnest the problems connected with air-raid defence. A sufficient number of Air-raid Wardens to take charge of areas in the event of a raid, under the control of a Chief Air-raid Warden are also required. *(WSG)*

An ARP bureau and training centre was subsequently opened at Colebrook House on the Esplanade, which had been 'smartened up considerably to make it habitable'. One hundred and fifty volunteer ARP wardens were also recruited.

Air-raid siren tests took place throughout Sussex, although even at this late stage opposition to them was being voiced. Battle Rural District Council's decision to provide a siren at Robertsbridge was met with strong opposition:

Presumably we will have to pay for it and yet we have had nothing to say about it', voiced the Salehurst Parish Council, 'we don't think it is necessary, it is perfectly ridiculous and they have not taken any notice of the people who do not want it. *(SX EXP)*

Throughout Sussex, air-raid precautions were in hand. Arundel had converted the basement of its town hall into an air-raid shelter, including installing electric light to this and the ground floor, which was converted into a first aid station for men. Other places in the town were also earmarked for first aid posts. At Worthing an ARP officer was appointed at a salary of £350 per annum. His duties were to serve both Arundel and Worthing with a portion of his salary paid by both. Littlehampton trained up twenty-six special constables in ARP work. West Sussex Council also enclosed a circular, printed in red, with their rate demands, appealing for more voluntary co-operation from townsfolk to assist the ARP.

At Cuckfield, the Council adapted a number of basement rooms and cellars as air-raid shelters for the use of people caught in the streets during a raid. Fingerposts were set up at various places to indicate where the shelters were.

An underground shelter at Broadwater Green, Worthing (West Sussex Library Service PP-WSL-WGP000037)

The nearby villages of Lindfield and Hassocks adopted the same type of defences, whilst at Burgess Hill, four large trenches were dug. The caves on the West Hill overlooking the Old Town were put to good use as shelters at Hastings, whilst at Lewes emergency shelters could accommodate more than 600 people, including those from the local chalk pit.

In July, the Ministry of Home Security issued a 3d (2p) pamphlet entitled *Air Raids; what you must know and what you must do*. This gave comprehensive instructions that ordinary men and women needed to know for their protection:

> The essential thing to do on hearing the siren or falling bombs is to take cover. No shelter, unless it is 50 to 80 feet underground, is proof against a direct hit, but the odds against a direct hit are tremendous. A cellar below ground level offers the best protection, but failing that a ground floor room is most suitable. The best place to sit in the refuge room is near a chimney breast, but out of line of the windows. If caught in open fields the best thing to do is to run to the nearest ditch and lie down. It is also advisable to plug cotton wool in the ears and hold a bit of rubber or a rolled up handkerchief between the teeth.
>
> In the event of an incendiary bomb raid, many fires will be started. An incendiary bomb had no great power of penetration and would probably lodge in the attic, or in the space below the roof timbers. Householders

should see that there is easy access to the attic, or through the trap door to the space below the roof and to see that all inflammable articles are removed. The best way to control an incendiary bomb is with a stirrup pump.

Householders were also advised to have their furniture and effects valued should they have to claim for under the Government Air Risks Compensation Scheme.

With the prospect of war looming ever closer, Sussex towns, to test both their abilities and the readiness of the emergency volunteers, staged exercises simulating enemy air raids, using the Royal Air Force, as this one in the Lewes area a few weeks before the declaration:

> Hostile aircraft will raid Lewes on Sunday morning as part of the ARP test which is being staged. They will circle the town at 300 miles an hour and may come over one, two, three or more times. *(SX EXP)*

The scenario for a full testing of the county town's defences was set, although there was opposition from two local churches, who refused to allow their premises to be used as wardens' posts on a Sunday. Despite this the exercise was a success:

> Lewes people can rest assured that the local ARP organisation is developing well and that we are prepared if there is an emergency tomorrow. *(SX EXP)*

The RAF also launched two mock bombing attacks on Hastings, where an ARP committee had been formed as early as 1935. The mock attacks were designed to test the command and abilities of the special constables, ARP wardens, St John's Ambulance Brigade, the Red Cross and the soldiers of the 5th Battalion (Territorials), the Royal Sussex Regiment. The first simulated a normal bombing, whilst the second was a gas attack. The exercises included blackout rehearsals and Hastings was plunged into darkness between midnight and four in the morning.

For the population the exercises required them to ensure that their windows and doors were completely covered by heavy blackout curtains, other dark covers or, possibly, painted over. These preparations had to be in place before sunset. ARP wardens patrolled the streets to ensure regulations were complied with. The streets were also blacked out with lamp-posts dimmed or switched off completely. Car headlights were covered with only a small slit of light showing through, traffic lights were similarly covered.

These exercises were reported as 'only a limited success', but as more took place over the county efficiency improved, such as the one conducted at Arundel at the end of June 1939:

The "action warning" siren will be sounded at 10pm. This will be a signal of two minutes duration, consisting of a succession of intermittent blasts of about five seconds, separated by silent periods of about three seconds. This warning will be reinforced by the Wardens blowing sharp blasts on whistles. On hearing this warning the streets should be cleared. People who can get to their homes within five minutes should do so and take cover. If unable to do so they should go the nearest shelter, the Wardens will advise where this is. All lights should be put out or properly obscured. It is suggested that this should be made an opportunity for everyone to take out civilian gas masks and try them on. The "raiders past" signal is the sounding of the siren continuously for two minutes. *(WSG)*

A major ARP blackout exercise affecting a large area of Sussex took place on the night of 8–9 July 1939. Handbills were issued to all householders in advance detailing their responsibilities and to assure them that the explosion of bombs and the lighting of flares to indicate where the bombs landed were harmless and not to get alarmed. The owners of vehicles were advised to keep off the roads during the darkened period, but if they had to drive, to proceed with their side- and rear-lamps only and not use their headlights unless really necessary. There were some amusing incidents during the exercise. A fireman at Burwash had to be rescued after falling into a river he did not see, whilst a warden unaware that his part of the exercise ended at midnight stayed at his post on a lone vigil until 5am, when somebody told him he should be home in bed.

All the preparations that had taken place throughout Sussex were now ready to be put into operation for real. Confidence was high as this report from Chichester on the eve of the declaration bears out:

The protection of essential centres has been practically completed and some three quarters of a million sandbags are being used in the directions considered necessary. The new County Hospital of St Richard's has been quickly prepared and equipped for use as an emergency hospital to relieve the London institutions by taking three hundred serious cases. The mansion in Oaklands Park, Chichester, is being transformed into an emergency isolation hospital in view of the possibility that the large number of evacuees may bring a certain amount of infectious disease with them and Chichester Corporation on Saturday bought two hundred blankets and earmarked six hundred more.

Goodwood House is being prepared for use if required as a military hospital. A number of its smaller treasures have been removed to safe storage, but the larger things, including Old Masters and the Gobelins Tapestry in the Queens Room cannot well be moved. Dale Park and Lavington House are preparing for use as emergency hospitals and billets for about one hundred expectant mothers are being found in adjacent villages. Stansted House and Petworth House are ready to take sixty and seventy refugees respectively.

The peace time blood transfusion service is being built up into an emergency service. The West Sussex County section is being taken over by the Women's Volunteer Service. In the Chichester district, which for this purpose includes the area west of the Arun, there are about eight hundred members signed on, of whom only about one hundred come from Chichester. At Horsham there are about three hundred and fifty and at Worthing about six hundred.

The Women's Volunteer Services are also undertaking everything they have been asked to do and its thousands of helpers, with members in every village are on their regular war stations. The meeting and distribution of evacuees, domestic work at the camps converted for children and canteen work for adult refugees, are among the services they are undertaking.

ARP services in Chichester City and Rural District are complete and there is a large quantity of food in storage. In the Rural District volunteers with clerical experience will be required for about a fortnight to assist with the issue of ration cards, of which about fifty thousand will have to go out. In the City the issue will be done by the Town Clerk's Department, with the help of the boys at the Secondary School. *(WSG)*

The Observer Corps was formed in the Great War and provided useful identification and warning of German air activity over Great Britain. After the war it was decommissioned only to be re-established in 1925, based in south-east England from Essex round to Hampshire. The Munich Crisis of 1938 led to the Observer Corps being mobilised for a week followed by an increasing number of exercises during 1939. Observation posts were constructed, located in a variety of places including hilltops, cliffs, on top of buildings, garden sheds, as well as new purpose built structures.

Manned by volunteers, the Observer Corps was mobilised on 24 August 1939. War was imminent.

A week later it was a reality. Germany had refused to pull back from invading Poland, ignoring the British ultimatum to do so. Neville Chamberlain, the British Prime Minister broadcast to the nation these famous words: 'Consequently this country is at war with Germany.'

Soon after the Prime Minister had finished his broadcast, air-raid warnings were sounded over Sussex. At the time many people were at their Sunday morning worship and were notified of the war announcement by their vicars:

> At Salehurst Church just as the Reverend rose to preach, a sidesman hurried up the aisle and whispered to him. The Vicar announced there had been an air raid warning and advised the congregation to leave and go home. The Doctor left in case of an emergency, but the service continued. Whilst at Robertsbridge no hooter signal was heard, the inhabitants being warned by police whistles and shouted warnings from the air raid wardens. *(SX EXP)*

At Bexhill the alarm caused some confusion:

> Whatever trials and tribulations await the people of Bexhill during the period of the war, it is unlikely that they will be called upon to undergo a severer nerve strain than they suffered on Sunday morning. The first air raid signal which dramatically succeeded the Premier's broadcast announcement of a state of war between Britain and Germany produced a feeling, not of fear or panic, but utter bewilderment. Half an hour had elapsed since the expiration of the British ultimatum. The enemy had apparently lost no time in sending his reply in a swift, devastating attack on our shores. Some people in the street began to run. Wardens appeared and directed everybody to take cover, advice more easily given than acted upon. They waited to see what was going to happen, until the "All Clear" signal relieved the tension and sent them indoors or on their several ways, thankful that Bexhill had not been bombed in the first hour of the war.
>
> Is Bexhill, after all the assurances of being a safety area, in the front line from the start? *(BX OBS)*

The emergency was soon over. It had been caused by an unidentified aircraft approaching across the Channel, which turned out to be friendly.

It was to be six years before Sussex returned to her peaceful days.

CHAPTER 4

Evacuees

With the prospects of a second war with Germany and the threat of heavy bombing raids on London and other cities, plans for the evacuation of schoolchildren to the safety of the country and seaside were securely in place when war was declared. Sussex and the south coast were considered 'safe' and hundreds of homes were visited in 1938 at the time of the Munich Crisis, by the Women's Voluntary Services, to ascertain in a preliminary survey how many children could be accommodated in

Evacuees Christmas party, 1941 (West Sussex Library Service PP/wsl/l001052/Wrens Warren Collection, by kind permission of Jill Tait)

the county. As the situation looked more serious, further visits to Sussex homes were made when each householder were asked whether they were willing to take children. If any refused, a reason had to be given. Although the scheme was voluntary, it was to be made compulsory if sufficient accommodation was not found.

Midhurst was quick off the mark sending a letter 'free of cost' to all the householders in their district:

In the event of war, children and some adults will be moved from the crowded cities to the less dangerous surroundings of the rural areas. To carry out the scheme successfully, careful arrangements have to be made. It will be remembered that a hasty investigation was made a few months ago to ascertain what accommodation is available in this district. It is now proposed to revise the record made, going more thoroughly into the case of every household than was possible in the pressing emergency of the former enquiry. The primary object is to ascertain in what homes lodging, board and care may be expected to be given for school children. Enquiries will also be made to ascertain what provision can be made for children under school age and their mothers. A visitor, duly authorised by the Rural District Council, will call on you shortly to make enquiries and it is requested that you will be so good as to give him/her every facility for carrying out his/her duties. *(SX EXP)*

Following this in early August 1939, Midhurst was one of several Sussex towns to conduct a comprehensive rehearsal of their evacuation arrangements, using children from the local grammar school:

The entire scheme, even to providing the one hundred and sixty school children, comprising the "evacuees" with buns and lemonade as refreshment, was gone through and all the children were dealt with in under two hours from the time of their arrival. *(SX EXP)*

Similar exercises then took place throughout Sussex. The coastal village of West Wittering, for instance, put ninety-two children through their arrangements reporting:

The smooth working of evacuation, should it ever become necessary, is assured in this village.

Under Operation *Pied Piper*, more detailed evacuation plans were publicised through the local authorities, transport arrangements were made with the railways and local bus companies, reception centres were set up and officials to run them appointed.

On 31 August, four days before the declaration of war, the government announced that the evacuation of schoolchildren and other priority classes from London would begin on Friday 1 September. This was seen as a preparatory measure, initial provision had been made for 78,300 parents, school teachers and children in Sussex. Towns and villages throughout the county indicated their readiness, with each local authority making its own arrangements for the reception and disposition of the evacuees, with compulsory powers for billeting them 'should any householders prove difficult'. Householders were to receive an evacuation allowance of 10s 6d (52.5p) a week for a single child and 8s 6d (42.5p) for each child if more than one was taken. This was to cover full board and lodging, but not clothes or medical expenses. Children under school age were accompanied by a parent or other responsible adult, who was expected to supply his or her own food, the householder receiving 3s (15p) for children and 5s (25p) for accompanying parents. In return, householders had to supply shelter, access to water and sanitary arrangements, plus cooking facilities. Any extra bedding required was requisitioned from government supplies.

The Mayor of Lewes urgently contacted the government to establish how many children the town could expect and whether they would be in school units with their teachers and would mothers of children under school age accompany them. In a rallying call he said:

> There has been much talk of the possibility of Sussex again being faced with one of those great emergencies which have always bought forth the best qualities of her people.

Bexhill's first arrivals came from Deptford and were mainly boys aged between 11 and 14. Only about half of the number expected arrived as a teacher explained it was the hop-picking season and a great many children at the last minute had preferred to go 'hopping'.

The second train to arrive bought a large number of toddlers, and mothers with babes in arms, mainly from Blackheath. Bexhill's scouts were on hand to help with the luggage being loaded onto lorries for transit to the reception centre.

The *Bexhill Observer*, in an editorial on the day the first evacuees were due to arrive, stated:

> By this morning, Bexhill will have many strangers within its gates and they will be followed by others as the evacuation of London proceeds according to schedule. Many are of tender years and others are expectant mothers and those affected by blindness.

LEAVE HITLER TO ME SONNY— YOU OUGHT TO BE OUT OF LONDON

It is only to be expected that among the children, particularly those of school age who have left their parents behind, there will be sorrowful hearts and the two classes of adults have also special claims to the sympathetic consideration of the townspeople. It will be Bexhill's desire as well as its duty to give them not only shelter, but a friendly welcome and I am sure it will not be wanting.

No one suggests that the scheme will not lead to some inconvenience. Householders who receive the evacuees are bound to find their normal routine of life affected in some measure, but our guests are now among us and the dictates of common humanity demand that we should do our best to make them feel at home.

Many of those who arrived had no idea where they were and asked whether they were in the country and were delighted to be told they were at the seaside, which most of them had never seen before. *(BX OBS)*

At Hastings, the first evacuee train that pulled into the station carried 250 schoolchildren. They were taken to the seafront underground car park, where they were fed before being sent by bus to the schools they had been allocated to under the evacuation scheme. The *Hastings Observer* reported:

> Hastings's paramount task at the present stage of the emergency which the nation has to face is concerned with the carrying out of the evacuation scheme. The evacuees have begun to arrive and the influx will continue during the next day or two. Nowhere in its emergency preparations has the town made more complete and effective arrangements and the initial stages of the work of receiving evacuees has gone on with clockwork precision.
>
> The children themselves bore bravely under the separation from their homes and parents meeting the situation cheerfully on the whole. Brothers and sisters clung together and all were loaded with as much as they could carry, knapsacks, little suit cases, brown paper parcels and of course the inevitable gas mask in its little cardboard case. Some of the toddlers brought their toys, hugging dolls and balls as they trudged cheerfully along, wide eyed with wonder at the adventure of it all, beside their teachers.
>
> Hearts will be opened to the little people, whom the demands of the hour have been taken from their homes and their parents. Hastings must make them and all other evacuees who are coming to town under the scheme thoroughly welcome. The children themselves have been asked to be cheerful and friendly, to do their best to make things run smoothly and to help each other in any little difficulties that may arise. We need not doubt they will respond. *(HS&STL OBS)*

A further train arrived later with old, ill and blind people, whose London premises had been commandeered as emergency hospitals:

> The evacuation of London school-children to Hastings, Bexhill, Battle and the surrounding villages was carried out smoothly and effectively. Trainloads of children were discharged at frequent intervals throughout Friday and Saturday. About three thousand children were received and quartered in Hastings, where a number of patients from London hospitals were accommodated. Battle Town provided homes for about sixteen hundred children and Bexhill seven hundred. *(WSG)*

Eastbourne had 7,400 schoolchildren, mothers and babies arrive over the weekend, 'even as the air-raid sirens sounded evacuees were getting off the trains.'

Over the next four days the official exodus from London continued. Other children, evacuated from Portsmouth, a prime target with its large naval base, were settled in West Wittering and the villages south of Chichester. Throughout September, 42,000 evacuees arrived in the west of Sussex.

Littlehampton received their 'wartime guests', around 900, who joined the considerable number of evacuees who were already in the town the children and their teachers walked to their allotted distribution centres to receive their rations and then a large convoy of private cars conveyed them to their billets:

> The evacuees were, generally speaking, received in a friendly spirit and the children and mothers are showing obvious pleasure at being billeted in a town with the amenities Littlehampton is blessed with. *(WSG)*

Nearby Arundel received 1,300 evacuees from Tooting and Wimbledon, who on arrival were ushered into a marquee staffed by Red Cross nurses and examined by

Dr G.W. Eustace before receiving their rations of canned meat, condensed milk, biscuits and chocolate:

A long line of buses waited in the railway approach and then seven hundred children, mothers and teachers were distributed to Slindon, Walberton, Aldingbourne, Yapton, Eastergate, Lyminster and Warningcamp, the remaining six hundred were conveyed to the Arundel Church of England School, where tea and biscuits were served by the Women's Voluntary Service. Eighteen billeting officers under Mr JJ Coe then took charge and by bus, lorry and private car the children and mothers were taken to their new homes. The Duchess of Norfolk and Lady Rachel Davidson were prominent among the helpers in this stage of the evacuation, each cheerfully driving her own car to and from the school to the various billets. *(WSG)*

Bognor Regis took its share:

With about five thousand children billeted throughout the district and a further eight hundred coming from Croydon on Monday, the town has become a cheerful place in spite of war conditions. The arrangements previously made worked very smoothly and complaints from any quarter have been few.

The railway station was a busy place on Saturday, when the bulk of the children arrived and were met by nurses and other helpers. The Southdown bus depot was stripped of motor-coaches employed in carrying loads of happy boys and girls to the distribution centres and the teachers and officials eased the task of the local helpers. Until things have settled down to "normal" war conditions youngsters will be more or less free to find their own amusements and while the Front, deserted by the usual crowd of holiday folk, has proved a boon to the youngsters, a certain number have been in and out of half made shelter-trenches or climbing up sand bagged protection, until called off by somebody in authority. The old house, known as the Den in Upper Bognor Road, which has been used as a school in recent years, is once more the home of happy children under the care of the local guides. *(WSG)*

The Borough of Worthing were expecting 19,000 initially, but received only 10,000, whilst the Worthing rural district was also 3,000 short. Three days later, eleven special trains bought the rest. Around 150 volunteers from the Air Defence Cadets were on hand to distribute the rations, consisting of biscuits, corned beef, condensed milk and chocolate, before getting the evacuees on their particular buses for the final leg of their journeys:

> Everything went off without a hitch, so smoothly that practically every one of the trains leaving the Station on each of the three days was dead on time. The children bewildered, quiet and perfectly calm, their discipline did much to make the evacuation a success.
>
> It has been a week of intense activity in the town, but everywhere there is evidence of a quiet determination to face difficulties and unwanted tasks with cheerfulness. On Friday began the reception of the little refugees from London by special trains running every hour. They came from Streatham Hill, Bermondsey, West Norwood, Gipsy Hill and Queen's Road, Battersea, by eleven trains to Worthing Central Station. The whole work of reception was a fine piece of organisation. All the trains arrived to time and after the passengers had detrained the trains went down to the cleaning sheds where they were efficiently dealt with and returned as part of the normal service to London. The children with the assistance of a large number of voluntary helpers, were placed on Southdown coaches to be taken to the distribution centres, Mr FH Mably directing arrangements by loud-speaker. *(WSG)*

The children soon settled in: 'Worthing beach has never seen so many children,' commented the beach inspector.

At Lancing, the evacuees 'were received with extreme helpfulness from every householder in the village, they had been met remarkably well and the kindness shown had been remarkable'. (WSG)

The Chanctonbury district received 1,000 more than they were expecting, including mothers and teachers:

'The residents of Storrington, Pulborough, Washington and Ashington responded magnificently, they gave every possible help. Billeting Officers had no trouble in placing the evacuees and some people who were not required to take children offered to take one and even two.' (WSG)

At Findon, more mothers with two or three children than were expected arrived, which caused a little difficulty but this was soon overcome.

Generally, the evacuation went smoothly, although there were some problems. At Henfield, more mothers arrived than were expected and had to be temporarily billeted in the parish room, whilst at Crawley, difficulties arose regarding Roman Catholic families who, at the request of the Corpus Christie Society, had to be billeted with families of the same faith. Some householders in Crawley flatly refused to have women in their homes. They had agreed to take the children, but 'no other woman shall use my house' was the answer the billeting officers were met with.

Laughton and Ripe in East Sussex were the only two places for miles around that did not initially take any evacuees. This was due to the poor water supply that came mainly from the wells, which had been tested and the water found to be unsatisfactory. Overall, the mid-Sussex evacuees fitted in well:

The huge new population which Mid-Sussex has absorbed is beginning to settle down; reports from the various districts state that billeting has been completed, though in some cases re-distribution became necessary. Community canteens and hospitals are working satisfactorily, welfare committees are now active and the authorities have in hand arrangements for educating the children. *(MSX)*

Finally, imagine the scene at Robertsbridge Station when the large detraining squad, consisting of billeting officers, St John's Ambulance, nurses, scouts and other sundry officials to meet the evacuation train, were surprised. It steamed round the bend and into the station where it halted. Out stepped just one small tousle-haired boy aged 12 who announced proudly that he was the evacuee. And he was. Others arrived later.

By the middle of September, the evacuations had been largely completed:

One of the first calls made upon the people of Sussex was in connection with the billeting of the evacuated mothers and children. The manner in which that work has been carried out is another triumph for the British voluntary system and the good humour of all concerned.

In unprecedented conditions and circumstances an operation of considerable magnitude has been performed with astounding efficiency. All round there has been a spirit of true co-operation symbolic of the National unity.

Before the settling down of the County's guests can be described as wholly complete it is obvious a few adjustments will have to be made. For while the first and major part of the scheme has been so completely successful, there are now occasional anomalies and difficulties which could not have been foreseen precisely. For these the Tribunals are functioning. *(SX EXP)*

That the evacuation had health benefits for the children was recognised:

The huge new population of evacuees which East Sussex has absorbed is beginning to settle down. Reports from the various districts state that billeting has been completed, though in some cases re-distribution became necessary. One of the beneficial effects of the evacuation is the obvious improvement in the general health of the evacuees, after just a week in the Sunny South, the pale faces of the town children have a more healthy appearance. *(MSX)*

All schools in evacuation areas were initially closed, whilst those in the reception areas re-opened as soon as arrangements for the education of evacuees had been completed. Continuing the children's education was a priority, but often a big problem in the country areas where children were accommodated in several villages, making the teacher's job difficult to exercise control over their scattered pupils.

Those evacuated in the towns also faced problems with their school premises. Beryl Bolton was evacuated to Bognor Regis from Clapham on 1 September 1939. Initially she was sent to school in Nyewood Lane, following a morning assembly in a nearby hall. Later her 'school' was moved to the Bognor Methodist Hall:

There were five classes in the hall and two infant classes upstairs, each in a tiny badly ventilated room. My own class of thirty was accommodated on a platform at two trestle tables and one card table. Even when it was cold, the atmosphere in the hall became unbearable. All the staff suffered with bad throats.

It was not long before Beryl was moved to the seniors, situated at South Bersted School.

(Beryl returned to London in January 1943. In the 1950s she arrived back in Bognor Regis as the headmistress of Westloats School.)

School accommodation in Worthing was boosted by the opening of a newly built infant school in Dominion Road, followed by the re-opening of the existing schools that had been closed for a few days. The school day was split, with local children attending from 9am to 1pm, and the evacuees from 1pm to 5pm.

The evacuees in Crawley, 'where many more had arrived than had been expected,' initially attended open air schools, at the War Memorial Recreation Ground. Similar arrangements were initially in hand at Haywards Heath Recreation Ground, where the girls from the Henry Fawcett School, which adjoined the Kennington Oval Cricket Ground, had open-air arithmetic lessons, speech training, PT and then popular nature walks.

At Hassocks, the popular Adastra Ground 'teemed daily with East End mothers and children, for whom the ground is a seventh heaven, the children delight in having such a wide expanse of grass to play on'.

Petworth evacuees being taught in a church (West Sussex Gazette)

For many evacuees, it was the first time they had been in the country and become familiar with farm animals. One London boy wrote a school essay for his parents entitled 'Beasts and Birds':

The bird I am going to write about is the Owl. The Owl cannot see at all in the daytime and at night is as blind as a bat. I do not know much about the Owl, so I will go on to the Beast which I am going to choose. It is the Cow. The Cow is a mammal and it is tame. It has six sides, right, left, fore, back, also upper and a below. At the back it has a tail on which hangs a brush. With this it sends all the flies away, so that they will not fall into the milk. The head is for the purpose of growing horns and so that the mouth can be somewhere. The horns are to butt with. The mouth is to moo with. Under the Cow hangs the milk. It is arranged for milking. When people milk, the milk comes and there is never an end to the supply. How the Cow does it I have not yet realised, but it makes more and more. The Cow has a fine sense of smell.

One can smell it far away. This is the reason for fresh air in the country. The man-Cow is called an Ox, but he is not a mammal. The Cow does not eat much, but what it eats it eats twice so that it gets enough. When it is hungry it moos. When it says nothing it is because all its inside is full of grass. *(WSG)*

The evacuation was generally successful and much appreciated by the school staff and complimented in the press. At Hassocks, where the St George-in-the-East Central School from London were billeted, the headmaster wrote: 'Please accept our very sincere thanks for the kindly and warm hearted manner in which you have received us into your midst'.

And at Haywards Heath with the St Matthews School, Westminster, in town, their headmaster stated:

'Your organised work and arrangements were truly marvellous and the reception kind and most touching. We do feel most grateful and trust that we shall prove ourselves worthy of the welcome you have given us.'

Although the vast majority of the evacuees settled in their new homes there were problems, whilst others were sent home for such things as smoking in bed and uncontrollable bad behaviour.

Some attracted the attention of the local police constable for offences such as theft and vandalism, as in Worthing when twenty-three boy evacuees ended up in the Magistrates Court accused of wholesale thefts from local stores. Among the shops reporting the thefts were Woolworths, Marks and Spencer, W.H. Smith, Walker Brothers, Wades Garage and Lacey's.

Two others were in trouble at East Grinstead, where toys were stolen from Gamleys, money from the sister-in-charge of the private house for difficult evacuees and three bottles of cider from the Crown Hotel, which they drank in a nearby field.

The evacuees, who came from either a Poor Law Institution or an orphanage, were given varying terms of probation.

For most evacuees, life in Sussex was a complete change, and this was reflected in some of the comments made by them about their new surroundings:

A little East End boy billeted in a doctor's house remarked, "Coo, what a clean bed", when he saw his room for the first time.

Another boy steadfastly refused to be a guest in a policeman's house and cried and struggled until a change was made in his arrangements. *(WSG)*

With the complete difference of lifestyle and surroundings many of the local newspapers reported humorous incidents, sometimes perhaps unfairly, as the children settled into their new lives:

East Grinstead girl evacuees having cooking lessons (PP/WSL/L001053 WRENS Warren Collection, by kind permission of Jill Tait)

Two brothers from Greenwich sat down to tea at a rather large family table for the first time. One observed to the other in a hoarse but very audible whisper, "Blimey, the same pattern is on all the blinking cups".

Their new bedroom was a source of wonderment to two very small girls. One of them looked around very carefully and finally inquired: "Ain't there no holes for the mice to come in?"

'The lady of one middle class family sitting down with evacuee children commented, "I don't know how on earth I'm going to feed you on 8s 6d a week." To which one small boy (being helpful) said: "You will have to go out to work like mummy does."

Mothers visited after a week or so, often assisted by the Women's Institute. At Burwash, their headquarters was set aside as a meeting place, where parents

East Grinstead boy evacuees tackle metalwork (Wrens Warren Collection PP/WSL/ L0001054 by kind permission of Jill Tait)

were supplied with tea and coffee, but they brought their own food, thus relieving householders from any expense. This arrangement continued every Sunday during December as evacuee parents travelled by coach to many of the villages in Sussex to meet their children in the run-up to Christmas. East Hoathly decorated the village hall for the parents and friends who arrived at 12.30pm laden with Christmas cheer. The day was happily spent partying and the visitors being entertained, arranged as a joint effort between the parents in Southwark and the teachers of the evacuated school. At Hellingly, a Christmas party was held to which the mothers of evacuees were invited, as many children would not be home for the festivities, although some would, a move criticised in some quarters:

It is learned with great surprise that the four hundred secondary school boys billeted in Lewes are to be allowed to return to London for the Christmas recess. While we appreciate the joys of this re-union of parents and children, we cannot help thinking that someone has blundered to allow such a vast number to return all at one time, whilst still making more evacuations … we can only trust that those in authority who are responsible for this wholesale return of children to a danger zone will realise the folly of doing so and of making the whole scheme an absolute farce. *(WSG)*

Concerns were also raised regarding the payment of the allowances during the period of absence and re-evacuation.

The General Post Office in Sussex reported Christmas being busier than ever, with the large number of evacuees that were in the county over the festive season: 'the number of parcels to be delivered made the work even harder.'

Throughout Sussex, sterling efforts were made to give the evacuees a happy time, obviously tinged with sadness at not being with their parents. As well as parties, trips were made to cinemas and pantomimes. There were also plenty of sweets and oranges to be attended to. In many cases the costs of these events were covered by house-to-house collections and donations.

At Winchelsea, a hospital for evacuated children was run by 'society women', including Catherine Sandford, an experienced nurse who ran three military hospitals during the Great War. By the end of 1939 the hospital had treated forty-three cases, 'including broken arms, tonsillitis and quinsies'.

Children, expectant mothers and vulnerable people were not the only evacuees Sussex received. With the threat of bombing in London, inmates from the large prisons were evacuated to the smaller country establishments for their own safety and as security against a break-out should their prison receive a hit. To accommodate these men, 120 Lewes prison inmates nearing the end of their sentences were released with travel warrants to their homes and enough money to last them for the journey, thus making way for 130 prisoners and aliens awaiting deportation from Wandsworth Prison. During their journey from London, two prisoners escaped whilst their coach was at the Chailey crossroads. One was recaptured almost immediately but the other, despite a thorough search by police, villagers and territorials, made his getaway. It was some weeks before he was recaptured.

Lewes prison itself was suffering from a shortage of staff and overcrowding and it was not long before an incident occurred when a prison officer was badly assaulted by one long term serving evacuee.

The situation at the prison deteriorated and a tip-off from an inmate warned staff that weapons had been hidden within the establishment in readiness for a riot planned for the following day. The ringleaders were believed to have been some of the Wandsworth evacuees, members of a West End gang, 'mostly men of the worst type', who incited others to rebel. A search of the engineering workshops revealed a cache of daggers, bayonets and sticks loaded with lead. The ringleaders were returned to Wandsworth and, although extra staff were drafted in from Wormwood Scrubs, the situation remained far from calm. *(SX EXP)*

CHAPTER 5

War days at home

Life at home took on different priorities with the declaration, one being the immediate instruction that all foreign nationals (aliens) belonging to enemy countries resident in the UK were to report to the police on a daily basis. Hotel owners found themselves confronted with a long form on which they had to fill in the details of all their residents, names, nationality, sex, date of arrival, full address and passport details. In the case of aliens their registration certificate numbers had to be included. All these had to be kept up to date and available for police inspection at any time:

> Every day now an almost constant stream of aliens, other than German or Austrian flows into the Police Stations of Brighton and Hove and elsewhere in Sussex, in compliance with the order issued during the weekend that they shall report daily. In addition they may not use any motor vehicle, other than a public one, or cycle and must not be out of doors between the hours of 8pm and 6am.

Then, following an order issued by the government that all aliens between the age of 16 and 60 had to be rounded up, the police forces throughout Sussex set to work:

> Members of Brighton CID were busy on Sunday, "rounding up" all male enemy aliens known to be residing in the borough. Fetched from big hotels on the seafront and humbler dwelling places, they were taken to the Police Station either by foot or in the flying squad cars. They carried rugs and suitcases and after examination of their papers were taken in batches in the "Black Maria" for internment in the district. The "round up" continued throughout the day, the total number interned being little short of one hundred. There were no "scenes" and some of the aliens confessed that this was what they had been expecting for some time. *(SX EXP)*

The gathering of the harvest was ordered to be completed with the least possible delay. Land Army Girls were on duty to assist the farmers and their farmhands, with soldiers drafted in to give additional manpower.

Blackberrying parties were organised throughout Sussex:

Every year blackberries, one of Britain's most plentiful harvests ripen in hedgerows and in rough uncultivated patches of land and every year thousands of tons of this delicious fruit are allowed to go to waste. The Ministry of Food appeals to teachers, to Captains of Boy Scouts and Girl Guide Companies and to other responsible adults to organise parties to go out into the countryside and pick blackberries. *(SX EXP)*

Another harvest was hops and the invasion of the East Sussex hop pickers. At Bodiam, for instance, hundreds of Londoners, mainly from the East End, used the few weeks it took as an annual holiday, earning extra money, as well as benefitting from the clean Sussex air; 'the British Tommy needs his beer, so let's see that he gets it.'

Most of them had arrived at the time of the Declaration and in spite of the critical times the pickers have retained their cheerful, lively, hard working selves, with many bringing their gas masks. As one woman said, "we never bother about the newspapers and wireless when we are here and as for the blackout, well, we are always tired enough for bed when it gets dark. We have always had a blackout at night in the hop gardens and that's the difference". *(SX EXP)*

Fears that their children would not be joining friends in the evacuation areas when they returned were summed up by one mother: 'No doubt arrangements will be made. If it comes to that we wouldn't mind staying here!'

The blackouts or Emergency Lighting Regulations, although having been used for exercises before the war, were now strictly enforced. Internal lights were required to be completely obscured, with no interior light visible from outside any premises. So strict was the lighting order that any member of His Majesty's Forces was authorised to enter the premises or board any vehicle or vessel and take all the necessary steps as may be reasonably required for its enforcement. The most common offences included lights shining from behind yellow blinds and above dark curtains, motorists who switched on their garage lights whilst putting their cars away and front doors being opened, thus allowing light to stream out from the inside.

Pedestrians could use hand torches, provided they were dimmed by the use of two sheets of tissue paper over the bulb or the aperture through which the light was emitted, and at all times the torches had to be pointing downwards. They were also advised to carry a white object such as a newspaper or to wear a white article such as a handkerchief tied round a sleeve to help drivers see them.

Earlier restriction of the use of motor vehicle headlamps were relaxed until masks were issued whose use was compulsory. Until then the offside headlamp bulb was to be removed and an opaque cardboard disk fitted behind the glass of the near side headlamp covering the whole area except for a 2-inch semi-circular aperture. All headlamps and torches were to be switched off immediately the air-raid warning was sounded.

Petrol was rationed. As from Saturday 16 September 1939, strict limits on private motoring were introduced via ration books. Cars were generally allowed between 4 and 10 gallons a month.

Ration books were available from the county halls and at local post offices, where excise licences were normally obtained. All applications had to be accompanied by the car registration book, and two ration books marked first month and second month were then issued, the quantity of coupons they contained varied according to the rating of the car. The coupons were only valid for the month of issue to prevent hoarding. These, however, were the days when a lot of motorists laid their cars up for the winter, so the effect was not immediate on all.

All those who required extra rations, taxi drivers for example, had to apply for supplementary supplies, to the divisional petroleum officer.

Some motorists converted their vehicles to run on coal gas, produced by equipment carried on a trailer, sometimes with a large gas bag fixed to the roof to carry it in. But the distance a car could travel on a bag-full was limited.

Many motorists were caught out by not having enough petrol coupons to get them home, as this lady seen on the Lewis/Brighton Road in early January 1940:

> An expensive looking car being drawn by a horse provided a sign of the times on the Brighton Road on Sunday morning. It was being led by a smartly dressed young woman and inside were several passengers trying hard to ignore the many stares. *(SX EXP)*

One government instruction that was very unpopular was the closing down of cinemas, theatres and other places of entertainment as an air-raid precaution. If one was hit by a bomb, large numbers could be killed or injured. However, most cinemas were re-opened within two weeks after staff had been trained to deal with emergencies.

Sports and other gatherings for the purposes of indoor or outdoor entertainment and amusement involving large numbers of people congregating together were also temporarily prohibited, but churches were exempt. However, chief constables were given special powers to prohibit the opening of any premises so situated that the audience might be exposed to exceptional risk in the event of an air-raid.

Hoarding immediately became an offence for anybody who purchased more than a week's supply of any food, apart from that which had been bought previously. This did not mean there was a food shortage, but food rationing was quickly introduced. A national register was announced at the end of September with every man, woman and child listed for identification and food rationing. Registration forms had to be collected in exchange for an identity card.

From January 1940, sugar was rationed to 12oz per person per week. Those engaged in the preserving of oranges for marmalade-making were entitled to a further 3lb of sugar for every 2lb of oranges, provided documentary evidence of the purchase of oranges was produced and endorsed. This amount proved to be initially inadequate, the Lewis Food Committee reporting that 495 applications had been received from those making marmalade, representing over 40 cwts of sugar! Beekeepers were also given an extra allowance of 10lb of sugar per colony between the months of December to May, but again, documentary evidence was required.

Meat was rationed from March when the government announced that the Ministry of Food was to become the soul purchaser, at fixed prices, of all fat stock, including pigs for slaughter. In the weeks leading up to this date, the ministry instructed people to register with their particular butchers, in order to

'Did he say he had sausages?' A queue at Mants Butchers, Bognor Regis (Author's collection)

ensure everyone had their fair share when meat rationing commenced. Meat rationing registration had to be completed immediately. The butcher a housewife opted to use was purely her own choice.

People who kept pigs for their own use, cottagers for instance, were given a permit to slaughter them for use within their household only. They were, however, required to observe the rationing rules and detach and cancel the appropriate coupons in their ration books.

Farmers had the scheme extended to other classes of controlled livestock within their farms and for those employees they normally provided food for. Some items were off ration, *viz* edible offal, tripe, liver, hearts, kidneys, tongue, sweet breads and ox-tails, but housewives were told to shop early as there was not an unlimited supply.

An adult's weekly meat rations were controlled by price, being fixed at 1s 2d (6½p). Sausages were not including in the ration until 1943, but were quite scarce. The rest of the adult's weekly allowance was per item:

Bacon and ham 4oz, butter and cheese 2oz, whilst margarine and cooking fat attracted an allowance of 4oz. In addition, each adult could have one shell egg per week and 2oz of tea.

The above were followed on the ration book by jam, rice and dried fruit, tinned tomatoes and peas, biscuits and, probably the most unpopular with the children, sweets and chocolate restricted to 2oz a week. Milk for normal adults amounted to a maximum of 3 pints per week. However, expectant mothers, babies, young children and invalids had 'priority' milk. In March 1940, tea was rationed, followed in July by margarine and the icing on wedding cakes.

In order to supplement families' rations, the cultivation of allotments was encouraged, particularly for potatoes and root vegetables. Plenty of land was provided by the local authorities, 'Dig for Victory' becoming the buzzwords. The cultivation of allotments had far reaching effects. Apart from the obvious increase in the food supply, home-grown produce cut down the amount of infrastructure previously used for food transportation, releasing shipping cargo space for war essentials, relieving congestion on the railways, and retaining much needed capital at home. It would also stop any German attempt to starve the country into submission. Rats and rabbits were a real problem, eating the produce as it was growing. The government passed the Damage by Rabbits Act to deal with them.

In response to the government's request for the cultivation of 20,000 acres of grassland in East Sussex, Harper and Eede Ltd, ironmongers and engineers of The Cliff, Lewes, released their stock of tractors to assist.

Later in the war people were encouraged to spend their holidays at Volunteer Agricultural Camps to help safeguard the country against food shortages. Farmers and farm-workers needed all the help they could get.

'It's hard work but it's healthy' was their slogan. Volunteers were paid 1s (5p) an hour and 28s (£1 40p) per week for their accommodation and food. Three camps were arranged in East Sussex, at Rye, which was male only, and Lewes and Haywards Heath, which were mixed. They opened on 1 July each year and closed at the end of September. With the volunteers giving up their holidays, they were promised a good social life in the evenings.

Under wartime regulations, a very great number of foods could now only be sold by a retailer who had the appropriate licence. Prosecutions for breaking the licensing regulations followed. In one instance, Battle magistrates summoned Mrs Ruth Payne, who ran a small shop in Baldslow on the outskirts of St Leonards, for such offences. She had been in the habit before the war of selling potatoes, green vegetables and tobacco and had applied for a licence to sell certain foods. The licence granted enabled her to sell only chocolate, sugar confectionary, potatoes and fresh vegetables, canned or dry. Two members of the Food Executive Committee made separate purchases from Ruth's shop. The first bought a packet of cigarettes and then asked for a pot of marmalade, which Ruth did not have. However, she offered and he bought a small pot of jam. The second visitor purchased a packet of tea. In her defence, Mrs Payne wrote that before the war she used to 'oblige' her customers but had not done so since the offences. She was fined £1.

In a more serious case, the proprietor of the Horse Shoe Transport Café at Hurst Green, Raymond Randall, was fined £8 with £2 costs for selling more sugar than he ought to with every cup of tea, contrary to the Rationing Act. His café was open twelve hours a day selling on average twenty-three cups of tea per hour, thereby exceeding the one seventh of an ounce of sugar per cup.

A scheme to collect scrap metal to help the war effort was introduced throughout the country. There was a shortage of iron and other metals so iron railings, pots and pans, old bikes etc, were collected by council workmen, scouts and the military, to be recycled into armaments ranging from bullets to tanks. Even now evidence exists in most towns of this happening, stumps of railings still in the ground being a good example:

We said goodbye to our second load of aluminium on Tuesday. The lorry full of pots and pans, hot water bottles, shoe trees and even an aluminium side-car, testified to the fact that Bexhill has certainly done its bit in responding to the Government's appeal. So far the amount of aluminium sent has reached a total of three tons.

A Ministry of Works van collecting scrap metal at Northchapel (West Sussex Records Office Ph4265)

Our grateful thanks to those who collected aluminium at the various depots in the town and to those helpers and the Boy Scouts who so cheerfully and willingly helped to load the lorries. *(BX OBS)*

Other restrictions also came into force. Train services were considerably curtailed as more staff enlisted. Postal deliveries were cut back for the same reason. Pictorial postcards and photographs sent abroad in the mail addressed to neutral countries were stopped by the censorship.

Homing or racing pigeons were not to be liberated, except under the written authority permit granted by the chief officer of police. Any dead pigeon or one unable to fly, to which any article was attached, which may identify it or contain communicating information, was to be delivered to a member of HM Forces on duty or to a constable at a police station.

An order was issued forbidding anyone to sound within public hearing any siren, hooter, whistle, rattle, bell, horn, gong or similar instruments, except in accordance with the directions for air-raid warning purposes.

The need for more coal became critical as the war continued. Coal supplies had to be cut during the summer months on the one hand and more needed to be mined on the other. This led to the formation of the Bevin Boys, the brainchild of politician Aneurin Bevan, to divert some recruits to work in the mines rather than enlist in the forces. There were many Sussex men who found themselves working down the mines. In June 1944, the *Sussex Express* featured five from Lewes, four of whom were selected by ballot, whilst the fifth had already volunteered:

Robert Martin-Cramp, of Sun Street, Lewes, was a compositor and very keen to enlist in the Army. He was a member of the Lewes squadron of the Air Training Corps before transferring to the Royal Sussex Cadets when a unit was opened locally, joining the band where he 'was in his element with the big drum'. When selected for the Bevin Boys he had already passed his medical to enlist in the Army, but the ballot changed that. Resigned to his position he told the newspaper reporter, 'someone's got to do it.'

Another ex member of the Air Training Corps who had ambitions to join the Royal Air Force was Kenneth Bridgeman of Garden Street, Lewes, who was articled to a local firm of chartered accountants. He had been working in the mines since April and after getting over his 'initial annoyance' at being selected, found the work of testing twenty-seven miles of travelling way and air-ways for gas, a thousand feet down very interesting.

Herbert Parsons, of Abinger Close, Lewes, was an ex member of the Royal Sussex Cadets and was 'fighting mad' at being selected for the mines. He too had passed his medical for the Army and was a member of the Lewes Home Guard, working in the meantime in a local shop. His family stated that 'he is upset at working down a mine, when his heart was set on joining the Army and fighting for his Country'.

Having passed his Royal Navy medical, an 'enthusiastic' part-time fireman with the National Fire Service, Albert Pollard of Mount Place, Lewes, received notification that he would also be going down the mines. He had served in the fire service for two years as well as being employed by the Sussex War Agricultural Committee on land drainage work.

A few days before his eighteenth birthday, Gerald Harmer, of Sun Street, Lewes, volunteered to go down the mines without telling his family, leaving his employment in an aircraft factory, 'somewhere in the South of England'. He wrote home to say that he was getting on 'pretty well' but found the boots 'very heavy'. *(SX EXP)*

Finally, the annual Guy Fawkes celebrations were cancelled:

For the first time since the end of the Great War the traditional Sussex Bonfire processions had to be cancelled. The blackout was the obvious reason, but with many Bonfire Boys having joined the Forces most celebrations were shelved until after the war. At Lewes, where the largest celebrations took place, the 5 November was kept alive by would be revellers who met in a local hotel bar, where a firework was let off on a metal tray with a dull 'plop' and paper hats and whistles were 'strewn all over the bar. So ended Bonfire Night 1939, which was a pity, Adolf would have made a lovely guy. *(SX EXP)*

CHAPTER 6

Dunkirk

With the British Expeditionary Force trapped with their backs to the English Channel, Operation *Dynamo*, the code-name for their rescue was launched. Lifeboats, pleasure craft and other capable vessels from all along the Sussex coast were amongst those who answered the call:

> On 29 May all fishing boats capable of crossing the Channel were requisitioned all along the Sussex coast for the purpose of assisting the evacuation of Dunkirk and the fishermen readily responded, handing over their boats at the port at which they were required to do so. *(SA)*

At 1.15pm on 30 May, the call went out for as many lifeboats that could be mustered to report to Dover, and the Sussex men swung into action. The Hastings lifeboat *Cyril and Lillian Bishop* left that afternoon with a 'scratch' crew, such was their haste. All boats had to be in harbour by sunset or they were likely to be fired on by the army. Having arrived off Folkestone and not able to make Dover, the Hastings crew docked there for the night, sleeping on the floor of the Seaman's Mission:

> Throughout Wednesday and Thursday an endless procession of small craft, mostly fishing boats and yachts could be seen making up-Channel past Hastings on their way to join in the great task of rescue. The Hastings fishing fleet consisting of ten boats arrived on Thursday and were taken over by the naval authorities. The Hastings lifeboat, *Cyril and Lillian Bishop* and the Hastings fire float, which sailed later, berthed in Folkestone Harbour at dusk and proceeded the next day to where the lifeboat, in common with lifeboats from a wide area was taken over by he over by the Naval authorities. *(HS&STLOBS)*

The next morning the crew found that all the lifeboats answering the call had been requisitioned and were to sail to Dunkirk, with either a Royal Navy or Royal Navy Volunteer Reserve crew. Despite protests, there was nothing the Hastings men could do. Neither could the crews of Eastbourne's *Jane Holland* and Shoreham's *Rosa Wood and Phyllis Lunn*.

The *Jane Holland* had a rough time when she was rammed by a motor torpedo boat and then machine-gunned by the *Luftwaffe*, which caused her engine to fail. The crew abandoned her and she drifted out to sea before being found and towed back to Dover for repairs, although it was to be another year before she re-entered service. On the other hand, the *Rosa Wood and Phyllis Lunn* successfully made three trips from Dover to Dunkirk. Shoreham's *Cecil and Lillian Philpot* had a charmed life. For four hours she was grounded on the Dunkirk beach before being re-floated and she rescued fifty-one soldiers.

The Sussex lifeboats all did magnificent work, employed with others from Kent and Essex, in ferrying men from the beaches to the larger ships waiting off shore, as well as picking up those who were swimming. It is not known how many men they saved, but the feeling of the disgruntled lifeboat crews left behind was that had they been crewing their boats, many more might have been rescued.

On 5 June, the boats were handed back to their crews and looked 'well used'. The Hastings boat, which had been freshly painted a week or two beforehand, looked in a sorry state, complete with a hole through her bow. There were also signs that she may have capsized and been righted during the operations.

The *Cyril and Lillian Bishop* had only been back in Hastings a few hours when the navy again called her to service, this time to go to Newhaven and then to St Valery on the French coast to evacuate more soldiers. However, after a short period of waiting for orders at Newhaven, the rescue attempt was abandoned, because of the problems in taking people off the beach at that location, and the boat returned to Hastings.

As well as the lifeboats some, 700 little ships, including some from Sussex, and over 200 warships also took part, plus seven Dutch coasters that had escaped the Germans' clutches when they were invaded, as did approximately 120 Belgian ships similarly obtained.

In all, more than 331,000 British and French soldiers were rescued, men like driver Herbert Thomas serving with the Royal Army Service Corps, whose home was in Ringmer:

> My lorry was struck by an incendiary bomb in a dive bombing attack. I jumped out of my blazing cabin, injuring my hand and arm and made my way across a thick entanglement of barbed wire, and reached a canal. I cannot swim and the water came up to my neck but I got across to the other side where I met an Officer. We journeyed together until we reached the beach from which the men from the British Expeditionary Force were embarking. *(SX EXP)*.

Even then his luck held out. Once aboard a ship he was sent below, a few minutes later the ship was dive-bombed and some of his comrades still on deck were killed.

Able-Seaman Field, a former officer at Lewes prison, was a crew member of HMS *Havant* which, after rescuing 6,900 troops was bombed and sunk at Dunkirk whilst on its sixth trip:

The Nazis seemed to make a special effort that day. They attacked for four hours, a bomb finally exploding in the engine room. I was on the bridge at the time and the ship began to list heavily. Eight men were killed by the bombs and twenty wounded, but a civilian ship came alongside and took the rest of us off. We were bombed and machine gunned all the way home, but nobody was hurt. We were attacked from the air, but it only needed a few British planes in the air to make the Nazis sheer off. *(SX EXP)*

Trooper Ronald Olly from Hastings described the journey across the Channel:

I had had neither sleep nor any rest for quite three days and nights when we embarked on a little paddle steamer alongside the jetty at Dunkirk. I don't remember the name of the steamer, but from the colours it was painted I think it was one of the pleasure vessels that had just come over for the job; it was not a regular war vessel.

We got on board without being attacked in daylight on Tuesday morning and put to sea. As soon as we were clear of the harbour we were heavily shelled. The decks were crowded and there was no cover. Every man behaved with perfect discipline and remained at their post. A steam pipe was cut by the shelling which lost steam pressure and the steering gear was put out of action.

Then we were attacked by a squadron of Messerschmitts, which dived and machine gunned the decks with murderous fire. They also fired cannon and sent incendiary bullets at us.

The men flung themselves down on the deck. There were many casualties; it was terrible to see pals dying and not be able to do anything about it. Our machine gunner was killed in the first burst of enemy fire, the wireless was shot away, but not before an SOS had been sent and within a few minutes the RAF planes had chased the enemy away.

We were able to proceed towards Dover and a destroyer came and put a Doctor on board to attend our wounded. A tug took us into Dover as we could no longer move under our own steam.

I was glad, over joyed, to be back in England again. Now I am anxious to get back to France and have another slap at the enemy. Man for man, task for task, plane for plane, we've got them whacked. All we want now is to get our equipment together again and get back to the fight. *(HS&STL OBS)*

On arrival in England, a major effort was made to get the soldiers to their homes. Many extra trains, some having waited for a few days, were put on to take them inland and at every railway station help was on hand, food, drinks and cigarettes passed to them as well as hundreds of postcards for them to write home to their loved ones with the news that they were safely home. Amongst the public at the various stations were also wives, children, sweethearts and parents looking in desperation for their men folk, or anyone who could give them news:

> The grime of battle was on their bodies; eyes were heavy with fatigue. Some were so exhausted that they could not take what was being offered to them. They had been bombed, shelled and machine gunned on land and sea after days of intense fighting, Some of them had had no sleep for three or four days and little if any food. But their spirit, the spirit of heroes remained.
> "We haven't started yet. Give us a bit of sleep and a brush up and let's get back. We'll get the Huns next time". *(K&SX G)*

Dunkirk Day was remembered by Dilys Collier, who at the time was teaching at the Arundel Church of England Infant School. Situated close to both Ford and Tangmere airfields, the whole school had to spend the day in their shelters:

> Dunkirk Day began with a tense silence everywhere. Our school at the time had eight classes, roughly three hundred and fifty children, probably more with the evacuees. Our headmaster, Mr. Wise, conducted morning service as usual, but beginning, not with a prayer, but a short address.
> "This is a very special day in our lives and I know you will all behave like English Ladies and Gentlemen. I know too, you will be very brave today, for the children of Arundel School are always brave. In place of our first hymn we sing the National Anthem."
> We then preceded to our shelters in the playground, armed with first aid boxes, torches etc. We had been sent a large box of buns given by a local baker and we took these too; also coats, hats, books and so on. We were to stay there until the all clear sounded. There was no all clear that day and we

sang and sang. They could all choose what they wanted and it was, "She'll be coming round the mountain when she comes". I can never remain unmoved when I sometimes hear it now on the radio.

They were, as the Headmaster had forecast, very sensible and brave and all through that long, long day, when they heard literally hundreds of planes over head and explosions in the vicinity of Ford and Tangmere, they all asked:

"Is it one of ours?" and I would reply, "Yes they are all ours, we are quite safe."

The next morning the staff arrived at school not expecting any children, but they were all there; at assembly that morning, Mr. Wise made only one reference to the previous day. *(CHOBS)*

Re-evacuation

After the fall of France and Dunkirk, with the Germans now poised just across the Channel, their searchlights clearly visible from East Sussex, the threat of an invasion attempt saw the re-evacuation of the little guests from London who had been in Sussex for about ten months. The first children planned to be moved from what was now the Front Line had been billeted in Rye, Hastings, Bexhill, Eastbourne and Seaford. Eastbourne sent 2,500 and Hastings 1,200 all heading for the safety of Wales, far away from the immediate danger zone. Altogether some 10,000 evacuees were transferred. Comparisons were made with their arrival ten months earlier, pale-faced and often poorly clad, and now they departed looking bronzed and fit:

> After their stay in Sussex many of the County's little evacuees are to leave for other parts. In those communities which have been protesting recently about the strain which the presence of their temporary visitors has imposed, there will be a more sudden and complete relief than any of them could have anticipated. For while there are cases where evacuees have brought little but trouble in their train, there are many homes where a sincere and deep attachment has grown between the hosts and their guests. To very large numbers the parting will be an occasion of real regret. Sussex has played a noble part in this work of caring for the children. Its inhabitants have shown a spirit of goodwill and hospitality that will forever stand to their credit. *(SA)*

Over the previous nine months, a loving bond had developed between most evacuees and their hosts, and many a tear was shed as the re-evacuation took place.

At that stage no immediate plans for the evacuation of local children had been announced, but following a series of air-raids on Sussex towns and villages, in which two people were killed, the prepared plans were put into action. The children of Eastbourne, Hastings, Bexhill, Rye and parts of Newhaven and Seaford were evacuated in the first week of July, followed a few days later by those in the West Sussex coastal towns on 12 July. Although not compulsory the government were anxious that parents take advantage of the scheme and register their children for evacuation to the safer counties of Hertfordshire and Bedfordshire:

> Inland areas are safer from bombardment and invasion and the districts to which the children are going are less densely populated than the places they are already in.

With the evacuation of schoolchildren away from Sussex, some parents applied to send their other children abroad for safety under the scheme sponsored by the Children's Overseas Reception Board. All the applicants had to be medically examined and the names of those successful were forwarded to the board for final selection. Five countries, Canada, Australia, America, New Zealand and South Africa, were participating in the scheme, the children being able to select their preference, Canada becoming the most popular. In Lewes, ten percent of children attending the elementary schools applied.

The Bec family from Bognor Regis opted to travel to Canada at their own expense and booked their passage on the SS *City of Benares*, which sailed from Liverpool on 17 September 1940, bound for the Canadian ports of Quebec and Montreal as part of a convoy. On board were ninety child evacuees along with their adult escorts. Dereck Bec, his sister and mother had retired for the night when just before midnight the German submarine *U48* fired two torpedoes, both of which missed, but a third struck the stern of the ship and she sank within half-an-hour 250 miles south west of Rockall.

HMS *Hurricane* came to the rescue about twenty-four hours later, picking up 105 survivors, including the Becs. They were the lucky ones. Many evacuees were lost when the ship sunk, whilst others died of exposure waiting in their lifeboats for rescue.

CHAPTER 7

The Sussex Home Guard

Although the likelihood of war increased in the late 1930s, the threat of an invasion of the United Kingdom was not taken as seriously as it might have been. There was a feeling that like the Great War, it happened 'over there', although the First World War gunfire of the battles had often been heard in Sussex. It was accepted that sporadic raids along the south coast were possible, but these could be dealt with by our forces based at home, with the Royal Navy and Royal Air Force both playing their part in support of the army.

However, with the fall of France on 22 June 1940, Great Britain stood alone, and with most of the BEF minus much equipment back home, the future looked bleak. Sussex was now the front line and fears of an invasion were on most people's minds, whereas before Dunkirk the general thought was that an invasion was unlikely. Fears that German parachutists would land in England, as they had in Belgium and Holland, were uppermost in many minds. Four weeks

Albourne and Sayers Home Guard, 1943 (West Sussex Records Office Ph16626)

earlier, the government, aware of possible German invasion plans, announced on 14 May the forming of the Local Defence Volunteers. At 9pm that evening in most households the occupiers were glued to their radios as Anthony Eden solemnly called for volunteers:

> I want to speak to you tonight about the form of warfare which the Germans have been employing so extensively against Holland and Belgium, the dropping of troops by parachute behind the main defensive line … these troops are specially armed and some have undergone specialised training. Their function is to seize important points, such as aerodromes, power stations, villages, railway junctions and telephone exchanges, either for the purpose of destroying them at once, or of holding them until the arrival of reinforcements.

He went on to explain how German plans were to cause disruption, disorganisation and confusion. The speed of any attack was a significant factor and the British response had to be 'prompt and rapid'. He appealed for men who at present were not serving in the forces and who wanted to help in the defence of the country to volunteer. Already, prior to this announcement, 'countless enquiries from all over the Kingdom' had been received and now was their opportunity:

> We want large numbers of such men, who are British subjects, between the ages of 17 to 65 to come forward to offer their services … when on duty you will form part of the Armed Forces, your period of service will be for the duration of the war … you will not be paid, but you will receive a uniform and be armed.

The response was immediate and overwhelming, those volunteering being instructed to hand their details into local police stations and wait until they were called:

> There has been an immediate response from all over the County to the broadcast appeal by Mr Anthony Eden, the new War Minister, for Local Defence Volunteers. The force which is entirely voluntary and unpaid will be used to defend the Country against parachute raids and volunteers will serve in their own localities. The service will not interfere with their civilian duties. *(SA)*

Enrolment began in Sussex on the following day, but in many places volunteers called in at their local police stations within a few minutes of Mr Eden's appeal. They included hundreds of ex-servicemen and many young men of 17 to 20 years, too young to enlist. Almost every walk of life was represented. Among the recruits reporting were old soldiers from privates to generals, some wearing their Great War medals when enlisting; having been through that war they 'knew how to shoot'. Some even 'forgot' just how old they were, with the upper age limit being 65. There were those who were 'over-age' but vehemently denied it.

The recruiting rush caused some administration problems as no command structure had been set up. This difficulty was solved utilising retired officers who had volunteered, senior local military officers and the Lord Lieutenant. Soon, local commanders were appointed, although in some places leading citizens had already organised their areas.

The Sussex response was magnificent, with twenty-six Home Guard battalions being raised, almost 9,000 men answering the call from the smallest hamlets to the largest towns, patrolling countryside and coast, ready for the invader.

The village of Storrington's unit was the first in the county to be formed, taking over a monastery that had been evacuated earlier. Haywards Heath reported several hundred recruits including Colonel J.R. Warren, the chairman of East Sussex County Council and a former officer commanding, the 4th Battalion, the Royal Sussex Regiment. He was joined by 'many who had a great deal of experience of war, the call for Volunteers has received an enthusiastic reception everywhere and still more are rolling in'. (SA)

Middleton on Sea Home Guard (West Sussex Records Office)

The Rural Dean of Lewes, the Revd. E. Griffiths, enlisted:

When the Corps met on Sunday the Rural Dean said there had been controversy as to whether clergymen should join the body or not, but when the order first came out he had made up his mind to join at once. His first command was to attend that morning and say a brief prayer. *(SA)*

In West Wittering, Mr F.H. Shaw recalled his first parade:

It started on Captain Hutcheson's tennis lawn and it was owing to the indefatigability of Captain Hutcheson and in spite of his tin leg that the Local Defence Volunteers were formed into a cohesive body, but only by degrees. I was introduced one delightful spring morning to its initial activities and told to join Corporal Boughton's Section. Corporal Boughton eyed me with a certain amount of nervousness and apprehension and said: "Of course, we don't know much about it yet," and we stood looking at one another until Captain Hutcheson's watchful eye obliged the Section into some sort of activity, so it marched round and round and up and down and we were started on a five years' experience. We learnt that to have a sense of humour was the most important thing in the world! Soon we learnt that our Platoon was part of a Company and that Company was part of a larger formation; and that larger formation was presided over by many high ranking Naval Officers and it was one or other of these Admirals who came to inspect and admire our military formations, which were entirely strange to them and sometimes even to ourselves. We were issued with armlets, badges and three denim uniforms for duty. Each night the guard assembled outside the Telephone Exchange in Cakeham Road, slipped the denim over their civilian clothes and carefully examined the hedgerows for possible German agents and malefactors, for suspicion was very much in the air and many innocent people were suspected of the darkest designs. *(WSRO)*

In the mid-Sussex village of Ardingly, 17-year-old Leslie Simmonds also enlisted:

About this time we were asked to join the Local Defence Volunteers. We all had to meet at Hapstead House one evening a week. Sergeant Major Hole came up from Ardingly College and started to teach us foot drill. We marched up and down Hapstead House drive and around the flower beds and although I say it myself, we became quite good at it. Soon after we had learnt our foot drill we were issued with our denim uniforms and our Ross rifles and bayonets.

These rifles proved to be very accurate. Sergeant Major Hole then started to teach us rifle drill, he was very strict: "Everybody, chins up, a-a-a-attention, up 1-2, across 1-2, away 1-2, up 1-2 across, down 1-2, stand easy". This was the shoulder arms; one had to be good at maths to cope with all this! *(WSRO)*

At the end of July the Local Defence Volunteers were officially renamed Home Guard following the term being mentioned by the new Prime Minister, Winston Churchill, in a radio broadcast a few days earlier. Often dubbed 'parashooters', they were poorly equipped at first, but with extensive local knowledge, they supported the regular army, using whatever they could find as a weapon from clubs to old rifles, broom handles with knives attached to the ends, to homemade bombs. Throughout Sussex, units were established, from Westbourne to Rye men, often after a day's work, patrolled the countryside and the important coastline, donning their uniforms, picking up their rifles and ammunition, which were kept at home, and reporting for duty.

As training improved and new equipment arrived, the Home Guard took on more responsibilities, including manning coastal gun batteries. The Bognor men captured a member of a downed Junkers JU88 and three more German airmen were captured by the Hastings Battalion, a year later the Billingshurst Battalion captured another one.

The Bexhill Battalion suffered an early casualty when, on 19 September 1940, a bomb hit and destroyed Jack Croft's home in Buckhurst Road. Jack was married with seven children, four of whom were evacuated at the time of their father's death.

In 2009 an unexploded bomb was found in the garden of the house next door.

Working within the ranks of the Sussex Home Guard, secret clandestine 'auxiliary units' were formed, highly trained men whose roles in the case of invasion were to attack and disrupt enemy progress, gather intelligence, and sniping. The men recruited formed a secret resistance, their existence unknown even to their families and comrades. Equipped with the best weaponry available, a regional headquarters was established at Tortington Manor House at Small Dole in West Sussex. The men recruited needed to have an intimate knowledge of their areas, farmers being well represented within the ranks. Throughout Sussex some twenty-five area patrols were set up, with hideouts from where the men would 'live' and operate.

In January 1942, the government introduced a form of conscription for the Home Guard, when all males between 18 and 51 were compelled to register for duty, unless already engaged in war duties. Hitherto, it had been operating on a voluntary basis. Numbers fluctuated with some members becoming old enough join the regular forces. Before compulsion was introduced, any member wishing to resign was given the opportunity. It was emphasised that the Home Guard's commitment to the defence of the country was growing day-by-day and there might come a time when the whole of that responsibility rested upon them, especially if the Expeditionary Forces were sent overseas.

Training took place with regular army units, such as this one that involved the Chichester Home Guard:

> Last week saw the close of a special fortnights training of the Home Guard and during this period the Chichester Company has had the full benefit of instruction from the Officers and NCO Instructors of an Infantry Training Centre, (ITC). "The principles of war," it is stated, "have been thoroughly taught". There have been demonstrations by the ITC of these principles as applied to the Platoon in attack and defence, reconnaissance and fighting patrols, application of fire and fire control, location of service targets, street fighting, defence of road blocks and other forms of modern warfare. In view of the fact that this voluntary training has taken place every night, including Saturdays and day time on Sundays, tribute must be paid to the zeal and keenness of all ranks of the Chichester Home Guard Company. *(WSG)*

Within Sussex several large concerns including the Southern Railway, the Southdown Bus Company and the General Post Office (GPO), formed their

Bognor Regis Home Guard (Author's collection)

own platoons. The Bognor Regis Post Office Local Defence Force was formed in May 1940 and initially recruited thirty-eight members, a mixture of postmen and night telephonists, joined a little later by members of the engineering staff, who set up a specialist signals system. Postman Arthur Batchelor, a retired warrant officer, was made company commander. The platoon's duties were to protect Bognor Regis Post Office and its property, including the telephone exchange, by mounting guards night and day. From July 1940, it became part of the 11th Sussex (39th) GPO Battalion, whose training was often in conjunction with the regular forces stationed in the area and consisted of arms drill, marches, bayonet practice and the firing of Bren guns and mortars. During air-raids they guarded the post office, mindful no doubt of their telephonist colleagues who stayed at their posts on the top floor of the building during these events.

They were active during the invasion scares on Bognor, including the nights of 6/7/8 September 1940, when they were 'stood to expecting to find Jerry coming over the Esplanade'.

On these three nights, it was widely thought that the invasion had begun. Home Guardsmen were called out from their beds and stood ready to meet the invaders. In some areas, church bells were rung giving an impression that the dreaded German paratroopers had actually landed.

The Southdown Motor Services Ltd were crucial. As well as their normal Home Guard duties, protecting company property, drills and exercises, their many omnibuses and motor coaches were to be used for the fast transportation of troops in an emergency. Consequently, a Motorised Transport Battalion was formed in

Post Office Home Guard, Bognor Regis (Author's Collection)

January 1941, eventually becoming known as the 12th Sussex (Southdown Motor Transport) Battalion and the Sussex Transport Column, with separate companies based at the various garage/depots in the county. Their transport role often carried them away from Sussex and eventually under more direct military control. The Transport Column was stood down at a parade in Brighton in 1944.

The Southern Railway Home Guard was formed in June 1940, becoming the 25th Sussex (2nd Southern Railway) Battalion. Like the Southdowns, they had a transport commitment as well as to protect Southern Rail property and the many miles of railway lines in the county. Anti-aircraft defences formed part of their duties with the carriage works at Lancing and the locomotive works at Brighton being manned, as were the junctions and depots at Horsham, Three Bridges and Lewes.

Thankfully, the Home Guard were never called upon to fight. But to the population of Sussex, the knowledge that these men were on duty, ready and alert helped them sleep at night. They were a good reassurance.

CHAPTER 8

Sussex in the front line

In the lead-up to the war there had been some defence preparation. Now, after witnessing the rapid advances of the German Army backed by their powerful air force, serious and urgent consideration to home defence took place.

A pamphlet entitled *Beat the Invader* was issued by the Ministry of Information in conjunction with the War Office and the Ministry of Home Security. It contained a message from Winston Churchill:

If the enemy lands or tries to land there will be most violent fighting. Not only will there be the battles when the enemy tries to come ashore, but afterwards

Soldiers erecting barbed-wire on Worthing seafront (West Sussex Library Service (www.westsussexpast.rg.uk) PP_WSL-P003402)

Bognor Regis Post Office being sand-bagged (West Sussex Library Service (www.westsussexpast.org.uk) PP_WS_-FLA_PO17)

there will fall upon his forces very heavy British counter attacks and all the time the enemy will be under the heaviest attack by British bombers.

The fewer civilians or non-combatants in these areas the better, apart from essential workers who must remain; so if you are advised to leave the place where you live, it is your duty to go elsewhere when you are told to leave. When the attack begins it will be too late to go and unless you receive definite instructions to move, your duty will be to stay where you are. You will have to get into the safest place you can find and stay there until the battle is over. For all of you the order of the day will be STAND FIRM.

This also applies to people inland if any considerable number of parachutists or airborne troops land in their neighbourhood. The Home Guard, supported by strong mobile columns wherever the enemy's numbers require it, will immediately come to grips with the invaders and there is little doubt will soon destroy them.

The final instructions given in the pamphlet were not to tell the enemy anything, give him anything, or help him in any way, but to give all the help possible to our troops.

The Sussex coast from Rye Bay in the east to Selsey Bill in the west contains many miles of flat land, split by the cliffs at Fairlight, Beachy Head and Seaford. If invasion came, German beach-heads were expected to be from Selsey to Brighton, Rottingdean, Newhaven, Cuckmere, Pevensey Bay, Bexhill, Rye Bay, Pett Level and Camber Sands. These flat areas were likely landing places that needed defending from the two German armies assigned for the task. The 16th, which would attack East Sussex from Camber Sands to Beachy Head, whilst the 9th would concentrate on West Sussex, from Brighton to Selsey Bill.

Under the command of Montgomery, based at Wiston House, the 3rd British Infantry Division were assigned to defend the Sussex coastline from Bognor to Brighton. Nothing was allowed to get in the way of their billeting arrangements. Whole villages and large parts of towns were taken over. Any properties in their path were demolished. The bungalow town at Shoreham, apart from the church, was raised to the ground, the residents were given just forty-eight hours to leave.

Under regulations passed in June 1940, Hastings, Bexhill, Rye and the rural district of Battle became defence areas. The effect of this declaration was to make it the duty of every person living in these areas to comply with any directions given by the regional commissioner. Three weeks later he declared that no person should enter these zones for the purposes of holidays, recreation and pleasure or as a casual wayfarer. Local residents were exempt. A few days later, similar instructions were issued in respect of Eastbourne, the urban districts of Seaford and Newhaven, the rural district of Hailsham and the parish of Peacehaven. Furthermore, no persons were allowed to proceed upon the Sussex beaches to the east of Bognor Regis, except when permitted by the local military commander, nor be on the sea front anywhere in the county during blackout hours. From 1 July, the Minister of Home Security declared all of Sussex to be a defence area:

> The public should recognise that directions of this kind are made for their protection and to enable the military to take all necessary steps to defend the country. *(SA)*

Cinemas and other places of entertainment had to close giving time enough for people to get indoors before the 10pm curfew was enforced from 28 July.

The only artillery unit in the county was defending the port of Newhaven and priority was given to boosting their numbers. Consequently, gun defences were situated at intervals along the Sussex coast and, although capable of shelling ships up to 7 miles away, they had little ammunition to begin with. They were manned by Territorial Army gunners initially, some using ex-naval guns brought back into service having been in storage since the end of the Great War, long after their ships had been scrapped. These gun batteries were installed at Bognor Regis, Angmering, Littlehampton, Worthing, Shoreham and Brighton, their combined arc of fire covering the West Sussex coast. Supporting these defences were guns in Oaklands Park, Chichester, which in turn were replaced by railway-mounted guns in the goods yard of Chichester Station, one of whose targets was RAF Thorney Island, which they would attack and deny its use to the enemy if an invasion began.

The line of batteries continued along the east Sussex coast from Brighton and the permanent Napoleonic Newhaven Fort to Seaford and Eastbourne. Further east, other sites were situated at Pevensey Bay (where a Roman Fort once stood, the Norman Castle having been built after the Battle of Hastings was again defending the country, with guns placed within its ancient walls), Normans Bay and at Cooden Beach, thus protecting the flat Pevensey Marshes. Bexhill and Hastings were manned where plans to set the sea alight were in hand should an attempt be made to land there. Another built at Cliff End, Pett Level, survives today in a remarkable condition. Covering Rye Bay and harbour, guns were sited at Winchelsea Beach and Jury's Gap, the most easterly battery being at Dungeness.

Probably the most secretive defensive assets were the underground tunnels of South Heighton Hill to the north of Newhaven. Requisitioned for the navy, becoming known as HMS *Forward*, they were an underground fortress that housed the most sophisticated communications devices available. So secret, they were not recorded with the Land Registry. They were excavated by the Royal Engineers and when completed, controlled ten coastal radar stations monitoring all maritime movements on and under the sea from Dungeness to Selsey Bill, the complete Sussex coastline.

Staffed mainly by WAAFs (the Women's Auxiliary Air Force) with WRAF (Women's Royal Air Force) and ATS (Auxiliary Territorial Service) assistance, the tunnels were operational until 1945. They were undetected by the enemy and largely unknown by the locals.

Many thousands of mines were laid right along the Sussex coast protecting harbours and river estuaries. Cuckmere Haven was considered by the Germans as an invasion point and was heavily fortified with dragon's teeth anti-tank defences, pill-boxes and gun emplacements. The River Cuckmere was also heavily mined and, in an attempt to confuse the *Luftwaffe*, part of the area was fitted with lights to make German pilots think they were over nearby Newhaven.

Large barbed-wire structures were put along the Sussex seafronts with the dual role of stopping people from using the beaches and hinder any invasion attempt.

Anti-landing obstacles at Goring by Sea. (West Sussex Library Service (www.westsussexpast. org.uk) PP_WSL_WGP001311)

More effective were anti-landing obstacles, constructed from scaffolding poles and supported by miles of dannet wire positioned at Bognor Regis, Climping, Lancing, Goring, Worthing and Brighton, where they were built in sections on the coastal fringe or manhandled and fixed in place at low tides, be they day or night. For the men constructing them it was dangerous work racing against the incoming tide.

Seven piers, built in Victorian times at Hastings, St Leonards, Eastbourne, Brighton, Worthing and Bognor Regis, often known as 'Palaces of Pleasure' were also seen as possible landing places for troops and supplies in the case of an invasion and needed disabling. In September 1940, the Royal Engineers were tasked with blowing up their central sections, thus denying their use to the enemy. Bognor Pier became a Royal Naval Observation Station and re-named HMS *St Barbara.*

Some early anti-tank defences were basic and 'home made'. It was doubtful they would have been very effective. Worthing, for example, had beach huts full of shingle and stones blocking roads whilst in other areas of Sussex, trees were cut down for the same purpose.

Thus, the first line of defence, often referred to as the 'coastal crust', was in place, its purpose to thwart any invasion and possibly delay any beach-heads developing.

If the coastal crust had been breached and the invading forces headed inland, further lines of defence had been constructed. Natural obstacles, such as the

Worthing Pier cut in half to prevent the enemy using it as a landing stage (West Sussex Library service (www.westsussexpast.org.uk) PP_WSL_WGP000023)

Defences on Bognor seafront (Frank L'Alouette Collection, by kind permission of Jeanette Hickman)

South Downs and the River Arun, then played their part. The Arun was too wide at its lower end for armour to cross thus forcing them upstream where existing bridges were defended by pill-boxes, anti-tank weaponry and concrete obstacles. Heavier guns covered the river crossings and if any British retreat had to take place these bridges would have been demolished before they fell into enemy hands. Further north another defence line with anti-tank ditches connecting the Rivers Adur and Ouse was constructed, their riverbanks were reinforced and built-up to give extra cover. Many hundreds of pill-boxes were constructed throughout the county. They were, in effect, reinforced defences for the use of infantry to hold off the advance of the invader. A 'stop line' of pill-boxes ran across the top of Sussex from Rudgewick in the west of the county to Peasmarsh in the east. Many more were scattered across the countryside, often singly, sometimes clustered together to protect a road junction, river crossings, bridges or some other strategically important area. These were known as Nodal Points. Examples of these were found all over Sussex.

The air threat also had to be considered with the Germans' possible use of troop-carrying gliders. The fields on the cliff tops were possible sites. These and fields further inland had volunteer diggers equipped with spades, shovels and pickaxes to dig trenches and then pile up the earth to make landings impossible. Other fields had old vehicles parked on them and wires strewn across them like washing lines.

In addition to the above, Sussexians had something else to protect them – the arrival of the Canadian Army.

In anticipation of the war, Canada had mobilised its Active Service Force consisting of three infantry brigades on 1 September 1939. They arrived in the United Kingdom during December, where all Canadian military forces were eventually designated the Canadian Army and were the largest force of Commonwealth troops ever stationed in the United Kingdom. They were quartered in Aldershot for training before the 2nd Infantry Division were deployed along the Sussex coast, where they spent many months. The defence of Sussex was in their hands, taking over garrison duties from the 3rd British Infantry Division. The 1st Infantry Division were also deployed in Sussex, among those stationed in Sussex were the Canadian Scottish and the Royal Winnipeg Rifles, at one time in Horsham, Storrington and Seaford. The Glengarry Highlanders were first stationed at Middleton on Sea in November 1941. From there, in 1942, they were spread out to East and West Witterings, Selsey, Thorney Island, Chichester and Horsham. The North Novas were in the Worthing area whilst training during 1942–44, and the Regina Regiment were familiar faces in Haywards Heath, Steyning, Bramber, Newhaven, Peacehaven and Horsham.

Other Canadian forces were billeted all over the county and were made very welcome by the locals. The population felt safe and children loved them. Many were stationed in Worthing where they laid minefields on the beaches, with large houses requisitioned for their accommodation and a gunnery school was established in Warren Road.

During 1941, they exercised regularly with British troops, initially in the defensive role but, as time went on and thoughts of a possible European invasion came to the fore the exercises took on a more offensive aspect. Practice beach landings were held at Bracklesham Bay, for instance.

In the summer of 1942, the 2nd Canadian Infantry Division set out from the Sussex ports of Newhaven and Shoreham as well as other ports in the Solent for a cross-Channel assault on the French seaside town of Dieppe, their objective to capture and hold the town for twenty-four hours before withdrawing. The convoy arrived off the Dieppe beaches the following morning and were met with such 'murderous enemy fire' that hundreds were killed as they left the landing craft, the beaches being littered with the bodies of the fallen. The raiding force was approximately 6,000-strong, of which more than 3,000 were killed, wounded or captured. As news of the tragedy filtered through, Sussex went into mourning; such were the deep feelings Sussexians had for their Commonwealth cousins, who had lived amongst them for the past two years.

A memorial tablet was unveiled at Telscombe Hall in October 1942, when members of the Canadian units who took part in the raid were represented. Messages were read from the king, the general officer commanding of the Canadian forces and Lord Louis Mountbatten:

A tribute to the memory of those gallant good hearted Canadian boys, who spent so many happy hours in this hall and who passed on while fighting for us in the Dieppe Raid on 19 August 1942; knowing what had to be done and doing it at all costs. They were worthy of their Country. *(SA)*

In East Grinstead, a Canadian wing was built in 1943 at the local hospital in memory of their aircrew who had died in the war. A Canadian hospital in Horsham sited in the old Horsham Union Workhouse opened in 1941 and was designated for D-Day casualties.

CHAPTER 9

The Battle of Britain

Following the fall of France, the Battle of Britain, which commenced in early July, was Germany's attempt to gain air superiority over the RAF, thereby clearing the skies over the Channel and southern counties, which would enable Hitler's invasion plans to go ahead. A great deal of action took place in the Sussex skies, which can only be touched on in this publication.

On Wednesday 3 July, enemy aeroplanes twice approached a south-east town, machine-gun bullets were fired and bombs dropped. In the second raid, bomb splinters resulted in the death of one man. During the day enemy aeroplanes were engaged by British machines off the coast.

On 12 August, the following happened at Mays Farm, Selmeston:

In an air battle on Monday 12 August over the Channel and along the coast a Nazi raider was driven down in a cornfield. The aeroplane a Messerschmitt 109 came out of a cloud and it crash landed in a field near a railway line. There were a number of holes in the fuselage, their positioning being a tribute to the accurate marksmanship of the British fighter pilots. Two railwaymen who were working about eighty yards away at the time observed the occupant jump out and commence to run immediately his aeroplane had come to a stop. He hid in the corn, but they immediately held him prisoner until the arrival of the military who took him into custody. *(SA)*

Anti-aircraft gun in Hastings town centre (Geoff Wolfe Collection)

Later that week:

> The pilot of a Nazi aeroplane abandoned his damaged machine in mid-air and made a parachute landing near a village on Friday where he was met by Miss Elsie Edye, who spoke perfect German and told him he was her prisoner. When she further told him that Germany had lost one hundred and forty four planes the previous day he could not believe it. She invited him to have tea while waiting for an escort, but before he could have the offered hospitality members of the Home Guard arrived and took him into custody. *(SA)*

There were two RAF stations, a satellite station and a Fleet Air Arm (FAA) base in West Sussex as the battle approached. Tangmere, to the east of Chichester, was used in the previous conflict by the Royal Flying Corps, before being handed over to the American Air Force and then mothballed. In 1925, it was re-opened, becoming operational the following year. With the prospects of war on the horizon, Tangmere was expanded in 1939 to defend the Sussex coast against the *Luftwaffe*.

During the early days of the war, RAF Tangmere became the main front line Battle of Britain airfield in Sussex, which saw a tremendous amount of action, and sadly losses, throughout the period. Close by a 'satellite' airfield at Westhampnett, a large flat stretch of land situated on the Goodwood Estate, had been requisitioned by the Air Ministry and developed as an emergency landing ground (ELG), but had been upgraded to a fighter station as well as a diversion for Tangmere, becoming operational on 8 August.

On 15 August, RAF Tangmere was attacked, although damage that day was fairly light. However, at 1pm on the following day, Junkers JU87 Stukas almost obliterated the airfield. Hangers, accommodation, the sick bay, parked aircraft and vehicles were destroyed, as was an air-raid shelter. Damage was also sustained by the station's power supply, water and sanitation systems. The attack sadly took the lives of thirteen servicemen and women, with a further twenty personnel wounded. In reply, Tangmere-based Hurricanes returning to their base shot down a fair number of the enemy. But despite the attack, Tangmere stayed operational throughout the Battle of Britain.

A little to the east, close to Littlehampton, was Ford, another Great War airfield, which had been in civil use during the interim period. This was also acquired and re-activated as part of the RAF expansion scheme of the late 1930s. New buildings, hangers and accommodation were constructed, and the station was handed over to the Fleet Air Arm and designated HMS *Peregrine*, as it was used primarily as a training base.

Ford Airfield under attack, 18 August 1949 (Frank L'Alouette collection, by kind permission of Jeanette Hickman)

Two days after Tangmere was hit, on 18 August, Ford also suffered a devastating attack when, in the early afternoon a formation of Stukas dive-bombed the airfield destroying buildings, hangers and fuel dumps, the thick black smoke being seen for miles around. Hurricanes and Spitfires from Tangmere and Westhampnett came to assist and accounted for three Stukas as they were returning home. Ford was in a state of devastation, thirteen aircraft were destroyed, with another twenty-three badly damaged. There was also considerable loss of life, twenty-eight naval personnel were killed, with a further seventy-five reported injured.

At the time of the attack the Fleet Air Arm were in the throes of moving out. The following month it became RAF Ford.

RAF Thorney Island, situated near the Hampshire border, was constructed in 1938 and received its first aircraft the same year. Thorney Island did not escape the Germans' attentions and was attacked on the same day as Ford. Stukas wrecked hangers and caused a massive explosion when the fuel dump was hit, but met with spirited resistance by some of the resident Blenheims that had managed to get airborne. These were joined by the Hurricanes and Spitfires from Tangmere and Westhampnett. In total, thirteen Stuka pilots did not return home that day.

Britain, however, had more to offer. Newly opened radar stations, known as the Chain Home Range, were positioned around the eastern, south-eastern and southern coasts, five of which were situated in Sussex, at Fairlight to the east of Hastings, Pevensey east of Eastbourne and Beachy Head to the west. Overlooking Shoreham by Sea, a little inland, stood Truleigh Hill with Poling to the east of Arundel. This was also attacked in the same raid that devastated

Ford. A sixth station, RAF Rye, although having the name of a Sussex town was situated just over the border in Kent.

Planned before the war in response to the ever-growing *Luftwaffe* threat, these were able to detect the enemy aircraft over a hundred miles away, thereby directing RAF fighters to intercept them long before they reached their intended targets. For their part, the Germans were unaware of their use, but being suspicious of their high aerials, made several bombing raids against them, which at times put them temporally out of action during the battle period. Pevensey and Rye were both attacked by Stukas on 12 August, with Rye's power supplies being disabled. On 18 August, Poling was badly damaged in the same raid that attacked Ford, whilst bomb damage to their power supplies again disabled Rye. Pevensey and Beachy Head were hit on 30 August.

In the skies over the county, dog-fights took place, watched by thousands of Sussexians. On the same day Tangmere was attacked, a big dog-fight took place in East Sussex over Bexhill:

The drone of engines was the first intimation that planes were about and machines flying at a great height could be seen darting in and out of the clouds. They appeared no bigger than a fly but were easily distinguishable against the blue patches of the sky as they were caught by the sun.

As they wheeled in and out intermittent bursts of machine gun fire could be heard; then, as the fight waxed hotter, the noise increased in volume and it sounded as if cannon firing planes were in action.

This phase of the battle lasted for a considerable time and there were reports of empty cartridge cases and clips showering down in some parts of the town.

An enemy fighter crashed to the ground. It was seen to fall from a great height with its engine roaring full out. The pilot left the machine, but apparently his parachute did not act and he was killed. The plane nose-dived deep into the ground. A local resident said that there was only "as much as you could put into a wheel-barrow above the ground". *(BX OBS)*

The *Shoreham Herald* described the dog-fighting that had taken place in mid-Sussex in its edition of 16 August;

People in the South-East Coast towns and villages had their first real taste of aerial warfare this week. On Tuesday morning (14 August) when dozens of German bombers and fighters crossed the coastline they could be seen engaged by British fighters. In that battle alone ten enemy machines were brought down and several pilots who bailed out were made prisoner. Several bombs were dropped, but little damage was reported and there were no serious casualties.

It was early on Tuesday that scores of planes could be seen in the brilliant sunlight, swooping and turning. Machine gun fire and the sound of anti-aircraft gunfire were heard.

In one village, two British fighters were seen chasing an enemy plane. Residents saw smoke coming from the German machine after the first attack and they saw the pilot leap from it, as it nose-dived towards the sea. The pilot landed a short distance away from a public assistance institution. He was injured and taken to the institution for attention.

Not long afterwards a second plane was bought down in the same area and again the pilot made a parachute landing and was injured. He was taken to join his colleague in hospital.

Further north a machine was seen to spiral out of the clouds and drift apparently out of control. It landed in a lake in a private park. The pilot was drowned.

One enemy fighter, a Messerschmitt 109, tried to escape from a Hurricane, by diving almost to the level of house tops. Hotly chased by the British plane it sped over villages and towns for a distance of three miles, but its fate was sure. A rapid burst of gunfire and it crashed into a cornfield. The pilot was unharmed and when the military authorities went towards him, he jumped from his machine, lit a cigarette, (which was later found to be of British manufacture) and cheerfully surrendered. He could not speak English, but judging by his broad smile he was happy to be safe on land. *(SH)*

Writing in the *Bognor Regis Observer*, 'a reporter' gave the following account of the activity he witnessed on 16 August:

Out of the blue came hurtling tons of sudden death, whistling and whining in a rising crescendo; in the space of five minutes, I saw the most terrific battle for supremacy taking place above me.

I saw a Hurricane and a Spitfire dive and half roll on to a Junkers 88 and literally blow him out of the air. The terrific fire-power of our fighters has to be seen to be understood. There is nothing that could possibly live in such a burst of fire. *(BR OBS)*

The attacks continued apace, this raid occurred on 18 August, as described by the *Mid Sussex Times* as a day of 'unprecedented excitement':

People sitting down to their Sunday lunches had the shock of their lives when they saw German bombers swooping from the direction of the Downs at such a low altitude that they seemed to just miss trees and house-tops. The swastikas on the planes could be clearly seen as the machines roared by. As the bombers, pursued by British fighters hedge-hopped over fields and houses, they heard the staccato sound of machine guns, also the dull thuds of bombs dropping. Although it was lunch-time there were a number of people in a park in a town over which the planes raced and many of these threw themselves on the ground. Others were not so wise and stood on the pavement looking up excitedly at the aerial monsters. Bullets from the machine guns bespattered shops and other buildings and it was thought that an unexploded bomb had fallen near a cinema, but a search failed to reveal anything. *(MSX)*

On 29 August, the *West Sussex Gazette* carried this article describing the shooting down of a German plane in the Chichester area:

Mid-August was here and in a remote corner of rural England the air of the afternoon was sultry. There were lowering clouds overhead and every prospect of a thunderstorm before the evening had passed. Standing on the terrace in front of the house, one looked north-west to the rolling wooded hills wrapped in a dark blue haze. In the distance could be heard the sound of reapers busy in the fields and still nearer sheep were grazing. Over all was the quiet of a late summer's day.

   Away in the distance could be heard the hum of aeroplanes growing ever nearer and nearer … The droning grew louder until the rising crescendo of sound seemed to make the very ground shake and tremble. Suddenly there was a burst of machine gun fire and through the angry clouds hurtled a plane, diving almost vertical to the earth, twisting and turning like something alive, with flames and smoke pouring from its engines and wings, the transparent nose of the fuselage one brilliant flash of red flame.

   We made a run for the house, shouting to those within to lie down and away from the windows. A dull crash was heard and after a few minutes the dreaded "crump-crump-crump" of bombs exploding and then the machine gun ammunition crackled away for some time and above that the crackle of a burning plane, with an ever increasing cloud of black smoke rising above the trees. We wondered if any of the crew had got out alive and the three of us started our way through the woods to discover the plane practically intact, but the nose burning furiously. We mounted a fence into the field and were about seventy-five yards away from the machine when the whole thing blew up with a blinding flash and a terrific explosion. We threw ourselves flat on the ground, whether or not we were partly blown down or not, I cannot say, but I, for one, have never measured my length quicker! As I went down I could see the plane going up in thousands of pieces and as I put my hands and arms over my head I felt something hot sear the flesh on my fingertips.

Lying there, with my ears deafened and my head ringing, I wondered what would hit me next; hoping and praying that it would not hurt too much! After a little while, which seemed like an eternity, I raised my head to see my two companions crawling on hands and knees for the shelter of a ditch. I followed and after settling down, gazed upward.

A few minutes later two Spitfires circled overhead to make sure that their work had been well and truly accomplished. We gave them a wave and with an answering salute they disappeared into the haze in pursuit of other raiders.

Oak trees and hedges had been blasted and were burning and there were small fires in many parts of the fields and woods around. Within a few minutes a warden and a member of the Home Guard were on the spot, with a few farm hands. It was discovered that one of the crew had bailed out, but that his parachute had failed to open. Of the rest of the crew, it need only be said that the explosion had carried out its grim task in an only too thorough a manner. *(WSG)*

As August drew to a close, many more raids on Sussex took place, although thankfully there were no more fatalities, but a considerable number of injuries. Several inhabitants of a village hotel were injured when two bombs fell close by. The force of the blast smashed windows, damaged doors and ceilings, blew a sleeping woman out of bed and a gentleman off his bicycle.

In another raid, members of the Home Guard on duty in the area narrowly escaped injuries when the casing of two bombs flew into their patrol, and a stick of bombs that landed in a field killed one horse and badly wounded another.

'MORE NAZI AIRPLANES SUCCUMB TO THE RAF' headlined the *Sussex Advertiser* in August as reports of further German losses continued. The following is their report of the activities in East Sussex during the first week of September 1940:

Once again Nazi aircraft have met with deadly opposition from the RAF and suffered heavy casualties at the hands of British fighter pilots, machines having been shot down in numerous places throughout the area during the past week.

Thick clouds of black smoke rolled over a Sussex village (Barcombe) on Monday afternoon when a Junkers 88 bomber crashed in a newly reaped cornfield and caught fire. While Hurricane fighters circled above watching their prey, three of the four crew in the plane got out and were arrested by the police. The crew of another bomber were taken prisoner when British fighters shot down their machine near another village on Monday.

Pieces of the wreckage of a German plane fell to earth at various places on the outskirts of another village on Thursday last week. The plane had been engaged by British fighters and after a short struggle was seen to make an almost vertical dive downwards. The plane flattened out and pieces of the fuselage broke away and fell into open country. A small part of the tail unit fell in the garden of an unoccupied bungalow, wrecking a rose bush and the engine crashed in a field at a poultry farm, but no damage was done.

One sightseer described the plane as being "crushed in mid air by a giant fist" and another told how he stood at his backdoor and "cheered without stopping until the wreckage hit the ground".

Local ARP units dealt with the situation promptly and the German pilot, who was injured and bailed out and was taken to hospital under guard.

On Monday evening a Dornier was brought down by a Spitfire in the Channel close to a coastal town. A man who witnessed the fight described how the German, pursued by the Spitfire, twisted and turned to escape out to sea. He said; "The Spitfire forced the Dornier down to escape out to sea, with sharp bursts of machine gun fire. The Dornier power dived and I thought it was going to hit the water when it started to climb. It was outmanoeuvred by the Spitfire pilot, who got underneath and gave a few seconds, burst of fire. There was a sharp explosion; the Dornier's magazine must have been hit. The plane came down in flames and hit the water but was flying too low for the occupants to bale out."

Bombs were dropped in various areas in the South East during the week, but there were no casualties and very little damage.

On Friday a large number of incendiary and two explosive bombs fell near one village, all dropping in fields and woods. The next night the same village had another visit from a raider, incendiary bombs being dropped, the only damage being a burnt out garden shed. A lone raider dropped high explosive bombs near a south-east town on Tuesday afternoon, there were no casualties.

Another lone raider visited a small South East town on Tuesday. The machine, a Dornier 17 appeared out of the clouds at a low altitude and dropped two bombs which fell in a small lane and in a field but caused no damage. Slight damage was done to a cottage roof near a town by one of several incendiary bombs and at a nearby village a cottage was slightly damaged by a high explosive bomb.

No serious damage was done when a number of high explosive and incendiary bombs fell in two hop fields, although a mother and three children had narrow escapes, part of the hedge in which they had been sheltering two or three minutes before being set on fire.

A farm worker who was walking across a field to pick up a burnt out incendiary bomb dropped the previous night, was met by a short burst of machine gun fire from a German plane which suddenly swooped down from low clouds, chased by a British fighter. The plane is believed to have been brought down in a neighbouring county a few minutes later. *(SA)*

The raids have had no ill effect on the people. In the words of a farm worker aged 70

"The bombs have given us a good idea of what to expect and now I feel more at ease than I did before. I feel that everyone has a good chance of not being injured." *(SA)*

From everywhere reports of the splendid work being done untiringly by the ARP and AFS are received. All their actions during the incidents have been prompt and effective and call for nothing but the highest praise. *(WSG)*

In a dog-fight over Hailsham in September, South African Flying Officer Percy Burton at the controls of his Hurricane ran out of ammunition whilst chasing a Messerschmitt 109 and made the ultimate sacrifice:

On Friday residents in a market town in the south-east saw an enemy aeroplane and an attacking British machine crash on the outskirts of the town. The RAF pilot appeared to ram his opponent deliberately.

Spectators of the incident heard fierce machine gun fire overhead before the two aeroplanes dived steeply from the clouds almost down to the housetops.

The Nazi pilot attempted to make off, when his opponent, after circling part of the town, appeared to ram the Messerschmitt deliberately, which crashed into an overhead sewer carried on tall brick pillars and parts of the machine were scattered over a wide area in fields near a sewage works. Both pilots were killed.

In the collision the British aeroplane lost a wing and it went on to hit a tree before catching fire. *(MSX)*

In mid-September, a graphic description of the action over East Sussex was published in the *Hastings Observer*:

Aerial battles over the South-East during the past week have bought heavy losses to the Nazi raiders, many being shot down. Residents in the districts concerned have hailed with delight these victories of the RAF.

On Thursday last during the course of a large scale engagement, two Messerschmitt 109s were sent crashing to earth within a few miles of each other not far from the coast, while another which took part in the same battle was seen disappearing towards the sea and losing height, obviously having been hit by the accurate fire of the British pilots.

Hundreds of people watched an exciting dog fight over a south-east district on Friday morning, which resulted in a German bomber crashing and exploding in a wood near a village. The enemy plane, pursued by a British fighter, disappeared behind the clouds and when it re-appeared it was crashing to earth in a spiral dive, minus a wing. The plane fell in a wood and a loud explosion was apparently caused by the bombs it carried. The wing fell in a ploughed field half a mile away. Two occupants of the plane bailed out and landed about three miles away. One was arrested by a member of the Home Guard and the other was quickly rounded up. The two other members of the crew crashed to death with the plane.

In another area the same day residents watched a thrilling encounter between Spitfires and an enemy machine. Black smoke was seen to pour out of the Junkers and three of its occupants bailed out, the other two, a non-Commissioned Officer and an airman were killed when the plane burst into flames. The descent of the three men who made parachute landings some miles from the scene of the crash was eagerly awaited by a Home Guard Platoon, who made a smart turnout. *(HA&STL OBS)*

Further German aircraft were destroyed over those few days, a Messerschmitt 109 in the Rye area with several others being bought down in the sea, their demise over being signalled by the returning Hurricane or Spitfire performing a victory roll, cheered on by the many onlookers.

It was far from one-sided. The RAF suffered its own losses and considerable damage occurred by the German bombers dropping their high explosive and incendiary bombs, often with delayed action.

By the end of September, the Battle of Britain had been won, Operation *Sea Lion*, the German code-name for invading England, had been postponed and Sussex gave a sigh of relief. But worse was to follow.

CHAPTER 10

The Sussex 'Blitz'

The first reported bombs to fall on Sussex occurred on Wednesday 22 May 1940, when a chicken farm received several hits on empty outbuildings, the only casualty being a pony grazing nearby. Many window panes were smashed and an empty stable destroyed. Forest Row was attacked two days later. Again there were no casualties, nor at Cowfold a week later when the first high explosive bomb was dropped at 3am on 29 May.

On 7 July 1940, the peace and quiet of a Sunday morning in Eastbourne was shattered by a lone Nazi raider approaching from the Channel. Unable to drop its bombs on any particular target because of anti-aircraft fire, they were released randomly, causing considerable damage and loss of life in the residential Whitley Road area.

Air-raid at Midhurst (West Sussex Records Office Ph 60)

Hastings' first attack occurred on 26 July 1940, when a German bomber dropped high explosive bombs on the West Hill area and the Hastings Cricket Ground. The casualties were one dead and two seriously injured. The bomber was being pursued over the town by two British planes and jettisoned its bombs in an attempt to escape.

Growing up in the town in the 1950s, the author well remembers the comments from older Hastingers regarding the cricket ground bomb and the damage to the strip, 'causing the start of the match to be delayed whilst they got the heavy roller out!'

Worthing was attacked on 14 September, when a German bomber dropped six bombs after circling the town at dawn. Premises were damaged, but there were no casualties. In another early attack, an aged lady was killed and three others seriously injured after a German raider dropped his bombs in the early hours of the morning. Three houses were destroyed and rescuers had to work whilst more German planes were flying overhead.

Two cinemas were bombed shortly afterwards. The Odeon in Brighton's Kemp Town was the first when, on 14 September 1940, a Dornier bomber in its bid to outrun the Spitfire that was chasing it, randomly released all its bombs hoping

Removing a 1-ton unexploded German bomb from underneath a church tower on 21 February 1941 (West Sussex Records Office PH16056)

to increase its chances of escape. Twenty 500kg bombs fell in the Edward Street and Upper Rock Gardens area of Kemp Town, with two making direct hits on the cinema full of children watching the matinee performance.

Four children lost their lives in the cinema, along with two adults. A further forty-nine civilians in the immediate area were also killed, with several hundred suffering injuries.

The Dornier that jettisoned the bombs was believed to have been shot down.

Just over two weeks later, on 30 September, the Hastings Plaza cinema was hit in a raid. The bomb exploded, killing eight people immediately with another six subsequently dying from their injuries over the next few days. Among the casualties was an airman home on leave to attend his brother's funeral, after he had been killed the week before in a previous air-raid.

Just before lunch on an October Saturday morning in 1940, the fourth *Luftwaffe* attack on Hastings that day took place when twelve bombs were dropped, one of which scored a direct hit on the Bedford Public House, which stood opposite the town's cricket ground in Queens Road. The Bedford was totally demolished, the landlord and his wife being rescued safely, but two others were killed, one being

Plaza Cinema, Hastings (The Geoff Wolfe collection)

a street trader who was working from his barrow outside the pub and buried by the debris. Close to the Bedford was a Marks and Spencer, whose trained ARP staff were immediately on the scene. In the same raid a man and lady had a lucky escape when another bomb exploded in the road close by, sending the van in which they were travelling up in the air and landing upside down.

By far the worst cinema raid occurred on Friday 9 July 1943 at East Grinstead. It was a wet afternoon and many people had gone to the Whitehall Cinema where a film starring the boyhood cowboy hero Hopalong Cassidy was being shown. In the audience there were many children, adults and Canadian soldiers. An air-raid alert notice was flashed on the screen and some people left for the shelters, but the majority remained.

Meanwhile, outside death was approaching in the shape of a lone Dornier 217 bomber, part of a planned attack on London, which had become detached in the cloud cover from the rest of its squadron. The crew opted to attack at random any likely target. First of all, it machine-gunned a train between Lingfield and East Grinstead before following the railway line to the town itself. Once overhead, the Dornier circled twice before dropping its load of two large 500kg bombs followed by ten smaller ones on London Road and High Street. Two of the bombs crashed through the roof of the cinema and, after a short delay, exploded, bringing down the roof. The cinema then collapsed on the remaining audience:

> Nearly all the casualties were suffered when a bomb crashed through the roof of the cinema into the "tenpennys", in which children were yelling excitedly during the screening of a cowboy drama. *(WSRO)*

The Bedford Hotel bomb site, Hastings (Geoff Wolfe Collection)

Whitehall Cinema bomb site, East Grinstead (West Sussex Records Office)

Almost immediately, troops and civil defence workers were on the scene searching for survivors. The bodies of the victims were removed to a nearby garage, which had hastily been converted into a morgue, to await identification.

The *Sussex Advertiser* reported the attack:

Late on Friday afternoon a small number of enemy aircraft crossed the South-East coast and two reached the greater London area. Bombs were dropped at different places. Two enemy bombers were brought down, one near Caterham (Surrey) and one near Sittingbourne (Kent) and both exploded killing the crews. A country town in the South-East area was attacked and a cinema was hit causing a large number of casualties, including many children. A twin engine German bomber swooped down out of low lying cloud, circled twice and then dropped several bombs. One made a direct hit on a cinema, another on an ironmongers shop, another on a builders and ladies outfitters and one fell near a factory. Others fell in the vicinity. The damage caused was considerable and there were casualties, some of which were fatal. In the cinema was an audience of one hundred and eighty-four, the majority being schoolchildren, who were trapped when the bomb fell. The bomb crashed through the roof into the front portion of the "house". Fire added to the horror of the scene. Many were buried under the fallen masonry and were killed instantly; others were pinned down and badly injured. A small number escaped with minor injuries.

Mr Herbert Breckpool, was at the time busy in his bake house at the restaurant next door, making jam tarts; suddenly the roof above his head split

Halton School, Hastings (The Geoff Wolfe collection)

open and through the opening fell the bodies of four women. Mr Breckpool, knowing that his eleven year old son was at the cinema, rushed to join the rescue workers, presently one of his colleagues came across the dead body of the boy. *(SA)*

The attack destroyed several other premises, including shops where people were registered to purchase food. Supplies of meat and groceries were rushed to other shops in order to deal with the demand.

This raid on East Grinstead caused the heaviest loss of life Sussex suffered during the war, with 108 people killed, of which forty-one were schoolchildren, including several sets of brothers and sisters. Of the Canadian soldiers, twenty-one were killed and a further eighteen were unaccounted for. The other fatalities were civilians. Another 235 people were injured.

However, the heaviest loss of children's lives life had occurred the previous year on 29 September 1942 at Petworth, when a German bomber, identified variously as being either a Junkers JU88 or a Heinkel 111, flew over the town and dropped three bombs. It is believed that its target was Petworth House. Two of the bombs missed their target but the third 'bounced' off a tree, ricocheted and exploded into Petworth Boys School, totally destroying it.

In the devastation, twenty-eight children lost their lives, as did the headmaster and an assistant teacher. Another twenty-four children were seriously injured and twenty-eight pupils survived the incident unscathed. A lady employed at the laundry close by was also killed. Canadian soldiers billeted nearby were quickly on the scene, as parents and others hurried to the school, many to hear the worst news.

The *Portsmouth Evening News* reported thus the following day:

The search continued today among the ruins of the school in a small town in the south of England which was bombed by a lone enemy raider yesterday.

Sixteen of the boys probably owe their lives to Miss Florence Weekes, of Portsmouth, who has been at the school about a year. When she heard the whistle of the bomb she gathered the children round her close to a wall which was the only part left standing after the explosion. Most of the children who answered her call escaped unhurt, but Miss Weekes was herself slightly injured and was taken to hospital. Another teacher Miss Moresby who was evacuated from London is also in hospital. The death toll now stands at twenty three; of these twenty are children, plus the headmaster and one teacher, the other being the manageress of the nearby laundry.

Digging went on all night. Nothing is being left to doubt and every single thing is being cleared away from the wrecked buildings. A Police Superintendent said:

"There are three unrecognisable boys' bodies lying in the local mortuary, but only one inquiry has been made ... I cannot understand why we have not heard about the other two boys, but as the day drags on no doubt we shall."

New facts of the tragedy were given by the Superintendent today. The headmaster Mr Charles Stevenson, first went immediately to the rescue of persons trapped in the laundry where the first bomb fell. A moment after the second bomb fell on the school and came to rest in a fireplace before it exploded. The headmaster shouted to the boys to run. Those who ran lived; the Head Master was one who stayed. The registers were destroyed, for the school had a direct hit, but it is known that the attendance was lower than usual. About 70 were in school.

Many of the children dived under their desks when the bombs fell. One of them, a boy named Morgan, pulled two of his companions under a desk with him, all of them got out alive.

The injured and the mothers of the town have shown a remarkable spirit, "the Battle of Britain Spirit" the Rector of the town called it last night. He has been visiting as many of the bereaved families as possible. He told the story of 11-year-old John Wakeford, whom he saw while the Doctors were treating him in hospital.

"Stick it, old boy," said the Rector and John despite his pain smiled back, "I'm one of the lucky ones, Sir."

Sadness reigns over the little town today, but the fighting spirit is still there. After the school was wrecked troops, firemen and rescue squads worked speedily and methodically to recover the dead and injured children from the debris. The rescue squads believe that several children are still buried. The Fire Brigade turned out with full equipment soon after the bombs fell, but there was no fire.

All through the day anxious mothers could be seen walking up to examine the lists pinned to a small notice board outside the casualty dressing station. Eighteen boys are reported to be missing. One badly injured boy included in the death roll of twenty-three died in hospital during the night.

When rescue workers reached a boy trapped in the debris, his first words to them were, "Where's my dinner?"

Petworth schoolboy William Herrington, one of the bombing victims, aged 7 (By kind permission of David and Davina Messenger)

The quiet country town came to a standstill a few days later when the school victims, including the staff, were laid to rest in a mass grave. The coffins were carried to the graveside by the same Canadian soldiers who tried so desperately to save the children. The funeral service was conducted by Bishop Bell, the Bishop of Chichester. The *Portsmouth Evening News:*

Twenty seven coffins containing the remains of victims of a bombing raid on a South of England boys

Canadian Army lorries carry the coffins of the victims to their resting place on 3 October 1942 (Garland Collection N 21855)

school were interred in a communal grave on Saturday, following a service at the local Parish Church.

The victims included the Headmaster of the school, Mr Charles Stevenson, his assistant teacher Miss Charlotte Marshall, whose coffins lay in the centre with a coffin each side of them containing unidentified remains. In the course of a brief address at the graveside the Bishop said that nobody there would ever forget Mr Stevenson, he was so devoted to his boys, nor his service to the Parish and Church where he was the organist. They will always remember how he and his assistant Miss Marshall, gave their lives at the post of duty.

The coffins, hidden beneath floral tributes, were bourne [sic] to the cemetery on fourteen Army trucks and soldiers were the bearers. The huge mournful procession was headed by the cross bearer, choir and clergy and included a great number of relatives, troops, Civil Defence and other services. On route it had to pass the bombed sight [sic]. Overhead the Royal Air Force provided an escort of fighters.

Two boys and the manageress of the laundry were buried at an adjoining village.

The children of the National School at West Green, Crawley, had a lucky escape on 4 February 1943, when two bombs were dropped at 8.30am on their school a few minutes before they were due to arrive. The lady cleaner was the only occupant at the time and escaped injury.

Five days later, St Mary's Catholic School at Worthing was attacked by cannon and machine-gunfire as the children were returning from lunch. Some children were rushed to the shelters in the playground whilst others were instructed to lie flat where they were in the building, although some on the top floor had no time to take cover and were wounded. One classroom was badly damaged, the teacher, Mrs Reed, despite being wounded by shrapnel, which hit a blackboard that fell on her, managed to keep the children safe. Speaking afterwards she said:

> We were cannoned from the front and machine gunned from the sides. We had never experienced anything like it before and the children, especially the tiny ones, were wonderful. They all gave a remarkable exhibition of self-control.

Two of the older boys were particularly brave during the attack. Thirteen-year-old Richard Mountain took charge of a class that the teachers had not yet reached, whilst Harry Roberts, despite being injured, managed to save the ARP register, in which the day's attendance figures were entered. Eight of the children as well as Mrs Reed were treated for shrapnel wounds.

Brighton and Hove had their share of bombing. One devastating raid on 25 May 1943 by up to thirty Focke-Wulf 190 fighter bombers saw twenty-one bombs dropped, leaving ten fatalities and over 120 people injured. The damage to property was considerable with around 150 houses being made uninhabitable leaving many hundreds homeless. The viaduct carrying the main Brighton–London line was also badly damaged.

The magnificent Royal Pavilion escaped any damage throughout the war. It was rumoured that if the invasion had occurred, it was to be Hitler's headquarters.

CHAPTER 11

Tip and run raids

Tip and run raids were exactly that, raids by fast fighter bombers that were made with increasing violence, targeting the Sussex coastal towns. Enemy aircraft would come in low over the Channel, evading the radar and 'tip' their bombs, followed by machine-gunning the roads and houses and then 'run' back home.

Bexhill became a tip and run victim on 9 May 1942, when considerable damage to property, including shops, a vicarage and houses, took place, but no casualties were reported. The attack was carried out by four Messerschmitt 109 fighter bombers, which approached directly from the sea.

Such attacks were a regular event in Hastings, a bad one taking place on 24 September 1942 when seven Focke-Wulf 190s fighter bombers escorted by a flight of Messerschmitt 109s flew low over the town dropping bombs in the lower St Leonards area prior to strafing the town with their cannons. The attack killed twenty-three people, including residents from the National Institute for the Blind home:

> Most of the patients in the blind home were in the rest room and were being taken to the shelter when a wing of their home received a direct hit. Some were trapped before they could reach the shelter and two patients were killed and five more, including the Matron were injured.
>
> One of the patients said; 'It was so sudden that we had no time to do anything. We were stunned for a minute.' *(HO)*

A further forty-three people were injured.

On 11 March 1943, another attack killed thirty-eight Hastingers with a further ninety people suffering various degrees of injuries. On this occasion, twenty Focke-Wulf 190 fighter bombers crossed the Channel and made landfall at Fairlight before turning west and, in line abreast, flew over the town at roof-top height, dropping their high explosive bombs randomly. They were supported by a further eight Focke-Wulf 190s patrolling close to the coast. This was the heaviest raid Hastings endured as far as death and destruction was concerned.

The worst tip and run attack on Hastings, damaging or destroying five public houses and hotels took place on Sunday 23 May 1943, when ten Focke-Wulf

190s swooped out of low clouds and flew across the town almost at roof-top height from the east, dropping twenty-five high explosive bombs and indiscriminately machine-gunning as they flew over.

It was just on 1pm and the pubs were very busy with lunchtime drinkers, some who, on hearing the air-raid warnings, were taking shelter inside. The first was the Swan Hotel, an old coaching inn situated in High Street, which received a direct hit and burst into flames being totally destroyed. Only one man and his dog survived the attack. One of the victims was William Hilder, the Hastings lifeboat engineer, one of the crew who took the lifeboat when it went to Dover prior to the Dunkirk evacuation. He had recently been notified that he had been awarded the Royal National Lifeboat Institution bronze medal for his actions, but his life was cut short and he never received it. The following day the bodies of the licensee Grace Gummerson and her 3-year-old son were recovered.

As the aircraft headed west a bomb bounced off the Queens Hotel and smashed into the Albany Hotel next door, killing some Canadian soldiers who were billeted there. On the attack went, towards St Leonards where their bombs hit three other hostelries. At the Warrior House, a resident and a hotel maid were both killed. The mayor of Hastings, who resided at the hotel, had left the premises a few minutes earlier. Another hotel nearby where a hundred people were having Sunday lunch

The Swan Hotel, Hastings, in more peaceful times (Author's collection)

THE SWAN HOTEL   c. 1880

had a fortunate escape. A bomb struck the top storey before crashing through into an adjoining building.

The next public house to be hit was the Warrior Gate, which received a direct hit and caught fire. The Tower, about ½ mile inland, was extremely lucky. A bomb ended up in the cellar but failed to explode. A department store and an antique furniture dealer's shop were extremely damaged and many houses were wrecked. Three churches also received blast damage.

As well as dropping the bombs, the raiders opened fire with machine-guns along the seafront where the anti-aircraft guns 'put up a tremendous barrage', and the raiders turned south across the Channel, where they were intercepted by RAF fighters who had arrived on the scene. 'More than one of the attacking planes were bought down.'

The raid lasted approximately two minutes and the casualty numbers were 'considerable', including a small number of children.

Eastbourne, probably the most bombed Sussex town, suffered badly. Raiders often approached via the shelter of Beachy Head, giving little or no warning. Apart from the high number of houses damaged or destroyed in various raids, the gasworks were set on fire, the electricity works badly damaged, as were the railway station and engine sheds. Fishermen in their boats off shore also attracted the raiders' machine-guns. The number of dead and wounded over this period was considerable.

A raid known as the Pub Crawl resulted in damage to two seafront hotels, the Gildredge and Cavendish, where an unexploded bomb became 'stuck' in the saloon bar doorway. The east wing of the Cavendish Hotel was shattered by a bomb dropped from an ME 109 on 4 May 1942. On 26 October 1942, the Alexandra Arms in Seaside was wrecked in a tip and run attack when it was hit by a bomb and then attacked with cannon and machine gun. No casualties occurred but several people were buried in the rubble and the Park Gates Hotel in Compton Street was partially wrecked in April 1943, when another hotel on the seafront was totally destroyed.

Focke-Wulf 190s raided the town on 26 August 1942:

Hit and run raiders, comprising two of Germany's latest fighters, Focke Wulf 190s, carrying high explosives which bombed a South-East coast town in a daylight raid on Saturday were clearly seen by many people in nearby villages.

The fighters came in at a low altitude over the sea, flew inland as they came, clipping the tops of tall Alder trees on one coastal farm and following closely the contours of the land. At one point they were so low in a small valley that although the sound of their engines were clearly audible, people in a village higher up could not see them.

Land workers saw the pilots in their cockpits quite distinctly, before both machines lifted to clear a hill and disappeared from sight. The sound of falling bombs was heard shortly afterwards. *(SA)*

An attempt by a raid on Newhaven to block the entrance to the port came close to succeeding when the port block ship SS *Davaar* was straddled by two bombs. The loss of the port would have been a serious blow.

One of the raids Worthing suffered was in August 1942, when two aircraft dropped phosphorous bombs, which burnt flesh badly and accounted for several Canadian soldiers who had just been stationed in the town. Worthing suffered again when, on 9 February 1943, an old lady and her invalid daughter lost their lives. Three days later, four aircraft 'in a lightning sweep' killed nine women, attacked an elementary school, injured several children and 'sprayed the streets with bullets'. The bombs they dropped damaged both commercial and private properties. Four weeks later, two people were killed when, in another attack, several houses were wrecked, 'rescue workers dug and tunnelled for hours for people believed to be buried in the debris'.

On the same day, two Focke-Wulf 190s flying in low and fast machine-gunned Littlehampton before dropping their bombs, hitting the congregational church manse and killing Revd Hailstone, his wife and friends. A week or two later, Littlehampton was to be heavily involved with the Canadians' raid on Dieppe

During the tip and run period, Seaford had its Southdown Bus Station bombed, which was showered by incendiary bombs, and a number of houses were destroyed. In all, twenty residents lost their lives during this period.

The small airport at Shoreham, although not a front-line station, came under attack from the raiding parties, and was bombed and machine-gunned on several occasions.

A typical tip and run raid took place on 2 February 1943, when three Focke-Wulf 190s crossed the Channel making landfall at Pett Level between Winchelsea and Hastings at 08:50am. Three buildings were strafed in Pett village before the planes travelled inland and attacked farm buildings at Westfield. Their next two targets were at Sedlescombe, where two cows were killed and a cottage damaged. The country town of Battle, the biggest target of their raid, received three 500kg bombs, which killed two civilians and injured twenty more. The FW 190s then headed towards Hailsham, another country town, damaging a farmhouse at Ashburnham and a barn, a cottage and another farmhouse near Herstmonceux on the way. On arrival they damaged five houses in the town and two more close by. Then they turned and headed south towards the Channel, following the River Cuckmere and attacking a house at Arlington. At 08:55am, they exited Sussex over the Cuckmere Haven, the raid taking just five minutes, damaging at least eighteen buildings, taking two lives and inflicting wounds on twenty others. It is interesting to read the report of the attack in the *Sussex Agricultural Express* three days later, which was obviously censored:

SOUTH EAST AREA GUNNED
On Tuesday morning a small market town in the south east and the surrounding rural area was sprayed with machine gun bullets and cannon shells from two or three enemy aircraft which flew over the district at rooftop level. Roofs and walls of a number of houses were damaged and windows were smashed, but the only casualty was a cow which was wounded by a bullet.

One farmhouse was hit by several shells and bullets and the farmer and his wife had narrow escapes. The former was shaving in front of a window when the missiles struck the house and one shell went halfway through the cavity wall only two or three yards away. His wife was in the adjoining room where bullets pierced the window. Two holes were made in the roof and tiles were knocked off the side of the house. In the garden a small tree was cut off near the ground by another shell. In the same locality the side wall of a cottage was partially holed by shells and bullets.

During the tip and run phase, the RAF lost a considerable number of machines and pilots, including many of our American allies, who were bombers going to or returning from raids over Germany.

As the tip and run raids died out towards the end of 1943, the *Luftwaffe* began a night-bombing campaign.

CHAPTER 12

D-Day

We are living and many dying, in the greatest event in the history of the world. Coming closely on the news of the capture of Rome, our people heard with bated breath last week that over 4000 Allied naval vessels, with thousands of smaller craft, backed by 11,000 front-line aircraft had crossed the English Channel; thousands of troops were being landed on the beaches of Normandy and that large numbers of airborne troops had descended behind the Germans.

Acting impulsively, or on the call of their King, not a few residents of Sussex visited the churches to pray; many more got into touch with the Throne of God from the privacy of their own homes. A sigh of relief went up when during the day that great leader, Mr Churchill, told the House of Commons that everything "was proceeding according to plan".

As our gallant airmen passed overhead making for France, as our brave sailors and soldiers went "into battle" the high hopes and benediction of the inhabitants of Sussex went with them.

It is certain that there is stiff fighting ahead for our Forces and there may be difficult times for the civilian population and while we have not the slightest doubt that the former will "do their duty" we are equally sure that the Sussex general public will also willingly endure whatever hardships that may befall them. *(SX EXP)*

Plans for the invasion of the European mainland were begun early in the war and Sussex was to be an integral part of them.

A successful raid was made on 4 June 1942, when Special Commando Troops landed in France between Le Touquet and Boulogne. Returning to England they disembarked at Hastings Harbour, where they were met by ambulances and covered army lorries that transported not only casualties to hospitals inland, but also a number of German prisoners, including a *Luftwaffe* officer to internment.

The rest of the troops were transported in open army lorries along the Hastings seafront giving the thumbs up as they went to the Adelphi Hotel in St Leonards. The following day they attended a cricket match at the Hastings central ground before returning to their bases.

The need for Advanced Landing Grounds (ALGs) was identified early in the war to disperse RAF fighter squadrons away from their permanent stations if they suffered damage or destruction from enemy action, and Sussex was ideally positioned to house some of them. Their ability to also provide attacking air support became obvious early in the war, when planning for the invasion of the Continent began. Thus, their locations near to the coast served the two purposes.

The ALGs were small, basic airstrips from which fighters or light bombers could operate. However, the sites proposed were generally on productive farmland, which did not please farmers and land-owners, who were under their own pressures from the Ministry of Agriculture to produce ever more quantities of food.

Construction was a mammoth task and completed in a relatively short time. Fields had to be cleared, trees cut down, hedgerows removed, as were farm buildings and, in the case of Chailey, the demolishing of the local pub.

Seven ALGs were constructed in Sussex, five of them close to Chichester. Apuldram, to the south-west, was one such site. With objections overcome and construction completed, the airfield received its first squadrons of Hawker Typhoon fighter bombers in the spring of 1942. These were used for a while to attack military installations in northern France before Apuldram was temporarily closed.

The airfield re-opened in April 1944, when three Czech Spitfire Squadrons flew in and were all active on D-Day. These were briefly joined by a Polish wing, but in November 1944 Apuldram was derequisitioned.

Further to the south, in the hamlet of Church Norton, a little known private airfield had been in sporadic use since 1930. In July 1942, it was requisitioned and became RAF Selsey, again in the face of Ministry of Agriculture objections as the new development embraced more land and the old priory, which became the officers' mess. RAF Selsey was the most southerly of the ALGs and became operational in May 1943, when a squadron of Spitfires arrived. These were joined a little later by Typhoons. Selsey was upgraded and, in April 1944, received more squadrons of Spitfires. Operations ceased in March 1944, although the airfield was not derequisitioned for some months afterwards.

Originally opened early in the war as an emergency landing strip for damaged aircraft, Funtington, to the west of Chichester, was upgraded to full ALG status in February 1943, with two runways laid. Two squadrons of Mustangs transferred from RAF Odiham and, leading up to D-Day, were employed on reconnaissance duties along the French coast. These squadrons subsequently returned to Odiham whilst further upgrading of the ALG took place. When it re-opened on 1 April 1944, Canadian pilots flew Typhoons in fighter/bomber sweeps over northern France, including attacks on suspected V1 launching sites. These terror weapons had not yet been brought into service. Funtington became very busy with several squadrons, including the Royal New Zealand Air Force operating Spitfires, Mustangs and Typhoons before it was closed in August 1944.

Merston Airfield was situated close to the Walnut Tree Public House at Runcton to the south of Chichester and was opened as a satellite to RAF Tangmere in 1941. From here, Typhoons and Spitfires operated until 1945, when it too was closed down.

Bognor Regis had an advanced landing ground built on farmland despite the Ministry of Agriculture's objections. Newspaper reports in early 1938 indicated that: 'land at Rose Green which the Council had proposed to buy unconditionally, has been acquired for a RAF Station.' Initial groundwork commenced in December 1942 and the airfield was officially operational on 1 July 1943, when three squadrons of Spitfires flew in. In preparation for D-Day, the airfield was upgraded, including hard-standing and several Blister hangers. Three squadrons of Spitfire IX fighter bombers, two of which were manned by Norwegians, were then based there, as well as Mustangs, ready for D-Day, when they were in action over the beachhead and flew sorties against V1 launching sites. After the invasion commenced, Avro Anson's and Dakotas of the Air Ambulance Flight were stationed there, ferrying wounded soldiers back from the fighting to be treated in the Royal West Sussex Hospital in Chichester and the Bognor War Memorial Hospital. Bognor Airfield returned to agricultural use early in 1945.

RAF Ford also received the wounded, whilst RAF Tangmere was continuously in action.

Supporting the invasion was RAF Bishop Otter College in Chichester, where a control unit operated commanding over fifty fighter and fighter bomber squadrons, plus an Air Sea Rescue Squadron.

Not all the ALGs were situated in south-west Sussex. Chailey lay to the south-east of Haywards Heath and benefitted from the natural cover provided by the surrounding woodland. The decision to go ahead with this airfield was made in December 1942, and by the summer the ground had been levelled, and two Sommerfeld Track runways had been laid, complete with their taxiways. The airfield then lay untouched except for grazing until the spring of 1943 when, in a flurry of activity, four Blister hangers were erected and three Spitfire equipped Polish squadrons took up residence. Over the D-Day period they were very active and later flew sorties against the Doodlebugs.

Both Polish and British airmen were stationed at Coolham, near Horsham, in another ALG, which became operational in April 1944, for about eighteen months, operating Spitfires and North American Mustangs. Only one or two permanent buildings were erected as the airmen lived under canvas.

Deanland, a little north-east of Newhaven, was officially opened on 1 April 1944 and had two Sommerfeld runways and four Blister hangers. The first residents were the Spitfires of three other Polish squadrons who were training in the fighter/bomber role. Being one of the larger ALGs, Deanland sometimes received visitors in the form of crippled aircraft returning from sorties gratefully using the airfield for emergency landings.

Friston Airfield was opened in 1940 and stood a little way inland from the Cuckmere Haven, functioning initially as an emergency landing ground. As the war progressed so did Friston's role, becoming a fighter station in 1942 with aircraft supporting the Dieppe raid. Damaged returning British and American bombers often landed there. Another ALG planned for Pulborough which had been an emergency landing ground since 1940, was never constructed.

All the above ALGs were flying sorties over northern France prior to D-Day, generally attacking anything and everything that looked hostile. They were all ready for the day itself, when their aircraft gave superb cover to the invasion fleet crossing the Channel.

D Day ships off the Sussex coast (Frank L'Alouette Collection, by kind permission of Jeanette Hickman)

The Sussex naval involvement were the ports and harbours of Newhaven, Shoreham, Littlehampton and Chichester, along with Poole in Dorset, which provided berths for an armada of landing craft. These would ferry troops from the large ships to the beaches of Normandy. These ports were given naval names, Newhaven, for instance, became HMS *Newt* whilst Chichester became HMS *Sea Serpent.*

Between the assembly for D-Day and the invasion, there was an intense period of maintenance, repairs, storing and provisioning. Hundreds of vehicles and armour were loaded at both Newhaven and Shoreham, which was also an embarkation port for British and Canadian troops, as well as hosting some of the invasion fleet. Its nearby airfield was also heavily involved, operating both Spitfires and another Air Sea Rescue Squadron.

In the months leading up to D-Day, Sussex became a giant military base. Tanks, armour, vehicles and artillery were hidden in well-camouflaged areas. Many thousands of troops were billeted throughout the county with marshalling areas at Bolney, Haywards Heath, Uckfield, Barcombe, Plumpton, Lewes, Brighton, Hassocks and RAF Thorney Island. All were camps billeting troops.

Worthing housed 8th Army veterans plus tanks, with Canadian and British Commandos billeted at Broadwater. Arundel, Angmering, Patching, Burpham and Clapham housed the USA 30th Division.

Littlehampton had a covert British detachment made up of volunteers from many regiments plus anti-Nazi Germans, soldiers from occupied countries, and Jewish men, all trained killers. Littlehampton was also to be an ammunition supply port.

Exercises took place inland as infantry units and commandos rehearsed the taking of villages and hand-to-hand fighting. Beach landing exercises took place at Climping near Littlehampton, and Bracklesham Bay. Heavy casualties were expected and an area at Sompting was developed as a hospital to receive both allied wounded and prisoners-of-war.

As D-Day drew nearer, visits to Sussex were made by the king, Winston Churchill and General Montgomery's double, who addressed troops at Broadwater Green, Worthing. General Eisenhower stayed in Chichester at the Ship Hotel whilst visiting the air bases.

Appeals were published in the press for the public not to embark on train journeys at Easter, which would hinder 'the transport of men tanks and shells, don't invade the trains this Easter!'

From 1 April 1944, the whole of southern Sussex, 'for reasons of operational security' was subject to a ban of visitors, with some exceptions. These centred around family visiting, taking up residence with a family of whose household they were usually members, or having been made homeless by enemy action and entering the area to live with relatives or friends. Other exceptions included becoming a patient in a hospital, nursing home or sanatoria, attending a university, college or school, or on necessary business 'which cannot be deferred'. Members of the armed forces and Merchant Navy were also exempt. The ban allowed those travelling through Sussex by train or coach who could do so only if they did not break their journey.

The penalties for anyone ignoring the restrictions were a fine of £100, three months imprisonment or both. It was emphasised that it was the responsibility of the visitors to satisfy themselves that they were in exempted or permitted classes and to carry documentation clarifying the reason for their visits. Everybody over the age of 16 had to carry an identity card. Binoculars and telescopes were banned.

At the end of May the Sussex roads were choked with military traffic and when the final signal came on 6 June 1944 thousands of troops headed for the embarkation ports.

Soon Sussex was 'empty'.

When the D-Day landings occurred, the Sussex Home Guard increased the number of patrols and posted extra guards in preparation for possible German parachutists launching counter-attacks. But as the invasion forces progressed, these threats diminished, as did the Home Guard's duties.

By August 1944, thoughts turned to whether the Home Guard was still required, although many urged it should be retained and 'stay alert until the all clear'. A Special Order of the Day issued by the commander-in-chief clarified the situation:

> The time will come when the Home Guard will no longer be needed to defend our Country from the invader. This may coincide with the end of the war in Europe, or it may be earlier.
>
> The decision must rest with the War Cabinet. But the time for this has not yet come. While there remains even the smallest danger of a Hun attempting to set his foot in this country the Home Guard will continue to be necessary and by its presence and efficiency will act as an essential insurance.
>
> I promise there will be no delay in letting the Home Guard know when they are no longer required; but until then-Carry On!

A week later the government announced the call-up of further entrants into the Home Guard was to be suspended with immediate effect. Compulsory drills and training were discontinued and such operational duties that were still required were to be carried out on a voluntary basis:

It was never the intention to keep the Home Guard on after it was no longer needed. Germany is in such a bad way that the General Staff has decided it can do without the Home Guard for the time being.

Within days the Home Guard were 'given leave' and stood down: 'They should, should the occasion arise, be embodied immediately, they have done a great job and now the chapter has ended.' *(SX EXP)*

Throughout Sussex final parades and dinners were held and the proud men returned to full-time civilian life with their heads held high. Stand-down day was 3 December 1944, with all members receiving a Home Guard Certificate that had been approved by the king, their colonel-in-chief: 'Large crowds turned out in the various towns and villages on Sunday to watch the stand down of the Home Guard's last parades followed by march pasts.' *(SX EXP)*

With the invasion progressing Sussex faced a new threat as death and destruction fell silently from the skies. The Doodlebugs had arrived.

CHAPTER 13

Doodlebug Alley

A brief period of relief and elation occurred after D-Day as the weary population looked forward to a quick end to the war. Their optimism was, however, short-lived, when Germany launched a new terror weapon, an onslaught that was to last three months.

A lady in Lewes wrote to the paper shortly after D-Day mentioning 'the robot planes which have been darting past our house lately'.

They were V1 rockets, also referred to as robot bombs, flying bombs and Doodlebugs, Hitler's 'revenge weapon', a pilotless plane that carried a ton of high explosives. Launched from bases along the French and Dutch coasts, their range was programmed by the amount of fuel they carried, generally enough to hit London, their main target. The direct routes they followed from their launching sites took hundreds of them over Sussex, predominantly in the eastern skies, their distinctive sound suddenly ceasing as the fuel ran out and they fell silently to earth, exploding with devastating results. They were capable of killing and injuring large numbers of people and destroying or damaging huge numbers of buildings and homes. Special instructions were issued informing the Sussex population what to do in a flying bomb emergency:

A V1 flying bomb, Doodlebug (Author's Collection)

Dwellers in Sussex who live anywhere near the flying bomb "lanes" are urged to be prepared for any emergency by making a mutual pact with relatives or friends living in another part of their town or district. Points that should be specially arranged for are:

"Accommodation if either house is damaged and the exchange of suit cases containing spare sets of essential clothing".

Pre-emergency plans by Sussex house-holders and other residents will greatly lighten the task of the authorities and play an important part in helping to defeat the flying bomb menace. *(SX EXP)*

The first Doodlebug in Sussex, and the second in England by just seven minutes, fell at Cuckfield on 10 June 1944, only four days after D-Day. Ten were launched in that initial salvo, but only four made it across the Channel. Of the others, two fell in nearby Kent and the only casualties occurred when the fourth one reached London, where six people were killed at Bethnal Green. A German spotter plane tasked with reporting the results met the RAF. The Doodlebug 'blitz' had begun.

One of the few in West Sussex landed in Madehurst on 12 July 1944; about 200 yards from the church, which had its windows blown out, and a number of other houses were damaged by its blast. The flying bomb was shot down by an anti-aircraft battery. It fell in the garden of a large country house and farm, uprooting trees, stripping fruit from an orchard, destroying a summer house and several bee hives, as well as blowing the roof off the house, bringing ceilings down and badly damaging the walls.

West Sussex suffered lightly compared to the east, with 136 falling there. Chichester remained Doodlebug-free, whilst nearby Bognor Regis had only one, on 27 August 1944. However, it did considerable damage, injuring sixty-five people and damaging more than 500 houses. An early one fell in Worthing, which landed in allotments. Nobody was killed, although some people were injured by flying glass and debris.

As the Allies advanced into France, those bases whose flying bombs were programmed to fly over West Sussex were captured and put out of action. Consequently, the majority of traffic flew over East Sussex until their bases were also captured.

London was the main target with many evacuating the city as the flying bombs did their work. In order to attempt to relieve their suffering false information was fed back to Germany that the Doodlebugs were flying over to the north of the city. This information resulted in the bombs being given less fuel, making them, as the Germans thought, land in London, when in fact more landed in East Sussex to the south. Sussex and Kent bore the brunt of the attacks, saving London from much devastation.

Many anti-aircraft guns originally sited on the North Downs were then redeployed along the south coast and grouped in areas under the Doodlebugs established routes. One gun-crew member, based in Hastings, was Winston Churchill's daughter Mary. When flying bombs were spotted out in the Channel, signal rockets were fired by lookouts indicating the route they were likely to follow over land, and the guns opened up with increasing success. The RAF attacked many hundreds with cannon- and machine-gunfire as they flew through the Sussex skies. They also soon developed the dangerous technique of flying beside them, using their own wings to gently tilt the wings of the Doodlebugs, turning them round to the direction from which they had come, or causing them to crash. Despite all these efforts, towns and villages throughout East Sussex suffered damage and casualties.

As the threat increased, the mayor of Lewes issued a statement on the importance of people of all ages to observe the air-raid sirens as a warning of immediate danger overhead:

I cannot emphasise too strongly the need for residents being alert and getting out of danger as speedily as possible on hearing the warning.

And Lewes householders living on the routes children walked to school were asked to open the doors of their houses when danger was imminent, thus giving the children shelter until the danger had passed. As it happened only one Doodlebug landed in the county town, whilst Brighton and Hove to the south remained completely untouched.

With the increasing threat of the Doodlebugs, another evacuation of children from Sussex took place, as the following from an East Sussex market town describes:

With a panting engine and coaches lined with little faces, an evacuation express pulled out of the station of an historic market town early on Tuesday morning with almost one hundred children aboard en route for the safety of places in Wales.

They came from half a dozen parishes in the rural district in which the station is situated, while at other stops the number was to be augmented by children from other villages, so that the train load comprised of some three hundred boisterous young passengers, before it really got under way on its cross country journey to Wales.

The scene at the station on the morning of this exodus was a cheerful one. Coaches brought the children in from the outlying villages and parents thronged to catch a last glimpse of their children and to wave "Au revoir".

They put on a happy face in the knowledge that, even though it meant a temporary parting, Tom and Janet and Rosemary were going to a place where Hitler's flying bombs are just something to read about in the papers.

The children waved. The train pulled out. The mothers departed and the station was quiet again. The children had gone, but they had gone to safer places, where the Germans latest savagery cannot harm them. *(SA)*

After a sixteen-hour journey the children arrived at Tenby, where: 'The whole town turned out to welcome the children and mothers who were taken to a rest centre and given a hot meal and accommodation for the night.' (WSG)

To the west of Eastbourne, the first flying bomb over East Dean was recorded on 13 June, with another shot down three days later. Others were bought down in the area, with damage sustained to a local school. Another, attacked off Birling Gap, caused damage to Friston Church. The Beachy Head lighthouse had two narrow escapes when V1s crashed into the cliff face adjacent to it.

Eastbourne received fourteen flying bomb 'hits', the first on 18 June occurred when a Doodlebug, already hit by anti-aircraft fire, fell and did considerable damage in the Charleston, Milton and Mountney Roads, where forty-one residents were injured. On 4 July, six houses had to be demolished and others were 'much damaged' in Astaire Avenue. Thirty-four people were injured in the evening of 27 July, when six more houses were demolished in Brassey Avenue, Hampden Park, and further houses standing in Baldwin Avenue were damaged during a late-night attack on 7 August. A week later the last Doodlebug to pass over Eastbourne flew by as, in France, the Allies captured their launching sites, thus cutting off this particular route to London.

Further east it was estimated that forty percent of the Doodlebugs directed at London crossed the coast between Rye and Bexhill, where it was further estimated that in one twenty-four-hour period, 485 flying bombs flew over the town. Inevitably, Bexhill suffered from the sixteen that fell in the borough, the highest number in Sussex. Damage was sustained by St Augustine's Church and in the Old Town, a convalescence home and the historic Bell Hotel.

The first sound of a Doodlebug over Hastings and St Leonards occurred in the late evening of 15 July. During the night, others were heard and one was brought down by anti-aircraft fire at Glyne Gap, a small area between Hastings and Bexhill, exploding between the railway line and the sea, damaging nearby property. But there were no casualties. Several others fell in the town causing some injuries, including one pursued by two Spitfires and an American Thunderbolt, which managed to successfully shoot it down. It crashed in the Sedlescombe Road South, St Leonards area:

A school suffered minor damage and four children were slightly injured, when a flying bomb, hit by an American fighter exploded in an orchard on Tuesday. The fighter had dived onto the robot's tail and fired a long burst. In the orchard the trees were stripped of their fruit and many were torn up by the roots. Four houses a short distance away were damaged and there were a few slight casualties due to flying glass. A church had some windows shattered and two people in a passing bus were cut by glass when the windows were blasted. *(HS&STL OBS)*

It was a different story three days later when a Doodlebug was brought down by a fighter over Hollington on a Sunday lunchtime, crashing into houses in Old Church Road, killing three people, with twelve other casualties:

Two men and a woman were killed, twelve people were injured and people were made temporarily homeless and had to be accommodated at a rest centre, when a flying bomb attacked by fighters over Southern England on Sunday afternoon, fell behind houses in a residential area.

Two houses were demolished, others were badly damaged and a number of others received lesser damage. A church and some shops in the neighbourhood were also damaged.

A great plume of smoke and dust hung over the scene after the explosion.

Civil Defence workers and other ready helpers at once began to clear away the wreckage which covered the roads, to make way for ambulances. Others dug among the debris and within an hour had extricated the dead people.

One of them had just been talking to his next door neighbours and ran indoors to take cover when the bomb fell. His house was left a heap of rubble. The neighbours, three men, went into a back room and although their house was severely damaged, none was badly hurt.

The Civil Defence Services went into action with great speed and efficiency and a rest centre which is kept standing by for any emergency was immediately put into use and proved of great value. First aid building repairs were also started very quickly.

Some of the homeless collected as much as they could and went in search of friends and temporary homes and a small boy tried a blast on his battered bugle which he had retrieved from his wrecked house.

Cricket players stopped their game to watch the flying bomb being fired at. *(HS&STL OBS)*

Another fatality occurred to the east of Hastings at Shearbarn Farm, when a Doodlebug crashed into a 40-acre ploughed field close to a farm cottage and exploded. The casualty, a middle-aged widow, the only occupant, was believed to have been in bed at the time. The Doodlebug was shot down by anti-aircraft gunfire from the seafront defences.

The last V1 to hit the town occurred at 11.40pm on 29 July, when it flew in low over the coast and crashed into St Leonards Parish Church, which lay back slightly from the seafront, there were no casualties:

On the debris piled high in front of the building could be seen the four chiming bells and the church organ which had been a gift to the church from the congregation in 1934 was hidden in the rubble. *(HA&STL OBS)*

A total of fifteen Doodlebugs fell in the borough, killing four people and leaving a further 114 residents with injuries of varying degrees and many properties damaged or destroyed.

AA guns on St Leonards seafront (Author's collection)

www.dengates.com

The ancient town of Rye had six hits. Another flying bomb destroyed the little church at Camber, whilst Major Hacking was killed in his home at Cadborough Farmhouse.

Inland, Doodlebugs fell in hundreds of locations in villages, towns and open countryside. The rural districts of Hailsham received 159, whilst the Battle District was hit with 374, almost half of the total that came down in East Sussex. Farmers suffered badly. One lost seventeen cows. Many farm buildings and out-houses received a good deal of damage, which caused a considerable loss of milk supplies in some areas.

When the fuselage of a Doodlebug that fell near a cottage in Westfield, East Sussex, was recovered it was set-up under a Union Jack and used to collect money for the Red Cross and did a good trade.

Two days later, at around 7.30am, a Doodlebug was intercepted by an RAF fighter over Sussex, which flew alongside it and 'tipped' the Doodlebug's wings, attempting to divert it from its course to London. Unfortunately, this action caused the flying bomb to crash and it exploded in London Road, East Grinstead. Ironically in the same place the cinema had been destroyed a year before, wrecking Sainsbury's newly rebuilt shop. The explosion damaged a further 400 buildings, with three people killed and thirty-eight injured. This incident prompted the immediate evacuation of local schoolchildren to safety near Aberystwyth in Wales.

The king and queen paid a visit to a number of anti-aircraft sites in the county and chatted freely to the men and women who were helping defend the country against flying bombs. During their stay, they visited the site in East Grinstead, the area that had been hit by a flying bomb a few hours earlier, described above.

On 4 August, in the East Sussex village of Laughton, a Doodlebug fell on three cottages, one of which was the post office, and completely demolished them. Five people, including the sub postmistress, were killed. She was the last Sussex V1 fatality. The Bell Inn was also damaged with every drinking glass broken. However, it was business as usual within a couple of hours, the landlord 'serving beer to the Civil Defence workers in tea cups'. (HS&STL OBS)

The Red Cross enlisted extra help for the aftermath of attacks by robot bombs, mainly ambulance drivers and storemen. On one day they issued more than 4,000 comforts and articles to victims of flying bombs. These included toilet kits, pyjamas, nightdresses and first aid requisites. Accommodation was also found for visiting relatives of victims who had been taken to hospital.

Boy scouts were also heavily involved, scrubbing floors, moving heavy furniture, sweeping up glass, soot, plaster and buckled lead from broken windows.

With the onset of the new football season in September, the government warned that some matches could be the subject of interruption from flying bombs and that 'spotters' should be stationed around the grounds to give warnings of their approach. If and when such warnings were received, the matches should be suspended and spectators, who should be widely distributed around the grounds, advised to take cover. But looking forward the local press added: 'It may be hoped that before the majority of Sussex Clubs open their seasons the danger of this additional excitement at football matches will have been eliminated.'

All the time, Allied forces were capturing the launch sites whilst others were destroyed by the RAF, and the Doodlebug threat diminished. Some were launched from mobile ramps, but by September the main threat was over, although the last one did not fall until 25 March 1945 in the East Grinstead area.

Figures published at the end of September revealed that of the 891 Doodlebugs that fell on Sussex, 136 were in the west, whilst 755 fell in the east. Many hundreds more fell in the sea around the coast, a lot of them close enough to the shore to do damage to property inland.

A new rocket, the V2, more powerful and faster, commenced attacks on England in September and, although the few that landed did considerable damage, their reign of terror lasted only a few weeks as they also had their bases overrun by the Allies. Only four fell in Sussex.

When the Doodlebug threat was over, the south-east defence commissioner stated:

When bombs fell in open country it often meant grave damage to cottages and in many cases whole villages went into mourning, but never a word of criticism or complaint was heard.

The people of Sussex have bravely shielded the people of London, who are aware of your spirit and are grateful. *(SX EXP)*

CHAPTER 14

Victory

As the invasion progressed there was a review of some of the wartime regulations; the blackout was relaxed with street lights again being switched on, but dimmer than usual. Households were exempted from putting up the blackout curtains, etc, at night, but with a warning that should the sirens sound then the previous conditions would be enforced. When it was finally discontinued, householders were encouraged to send their blackout material to a central depot, where it was used to make clothes for those suffering in France and Holland as well as providing material for the young girls in France who wore black pinafores. And the Women's Voluntary Services (WVS) encouraged its members to continue knitting warm clothing, with blankets and clothes collected for distribution in the liberated countries.

The Women's Land Army (WLA) continued to recruit, to maintain maximum food production. Volunteers were still needed for milking as consumption had increased.

Among those who 'volunteered' were parties of prisoners from Lewes Gaol, who by permission of HM Prison Commissioners, were helping with the war effort by performing agricultural tasks on various farms in East Sussex:

Removing anti-tank blocks from Worthing seafront (West Sussex Library Service PP-WSL-WGP000041)

These men who have been specially selected and give their word that they will behave themselves during their periods of liberty are conveyed daily to various farms and other places where there is agricultural work to be done and they spend all day in the open air, which is a pleasant change from working behind prison walls. They take their mid-day meals picnic fashion and so far have behaved very well indeed.

Only one prison officer was with them at the farm at Peacehaven where they have been working on potato sorting and all seemed to be enjoying themselves. They have done an extraordinary amount of good work, which no doubt has not only been a benefit to the Country but to the men themselves. *(SX EXP)*

Road signposts, withdrawn when invasion was a threat, were replaced in November 1944 and motorists were allowed to re-install wireless sets in their vehicles. Their cars no longer needed immobilising. However, concern was felt regarding the return to the road of many motorists and motor cyclists who had not driven or ridden for some years. The chief constable of Sussex issued the following advice:

They should study the Highway Code and its advice strictly followed. All vehicles should be carefully overhauled and all defects remedied, this precaution should save much trouble and inconvenience later and will remove a potential source of accidents. Road users must be vigilant; more traffic means extra care must be taken. *(SX EXP)*

Finally, motorists and motorcyclists were advised that police traffic patrols would be resuming, having been suspended during the hostilities.

Cyclists also came in for attention:

They are on no account to ride three abreast and in busy narrow streets to ride in single file. They must make their signals clearly and in good time and when riding should not carry bulky parcels on the handlebars. *(SX EXP)*

Despite the above warning, child cyclist accident figures increased.

Pedestrians were also given advice, being warned to remember:

That there would be an increase in traffic and they should not to be lulled into a sense of false security. When using the roads, they should make full use of the crossing places and carefully observe traffic signals, mechanical or otherwise

> Parents should make their children more traffic conscious and stress the dangers of playing in the road, taking hold of moving vehicles and crossing the road without first satisfying their selves that it is safe to do so. *(SX EXP)*

As Easter 1945 approached, many motorists were looking forward to a family outing, but were disappointed as there was no let-up in the wartime petrol restrictions:

> This was a disappointment to motorists and villagers who used to spend their holiday watching the cars drive past their homes.
>   Nothing less than an endless chain of cars on the London to Brighton road will convince Sussex folk of the restoration of something like normal times. *(SX EXP)*

At the beginning of May 1945, with victory in Europe imminent, the Home Office issued a circular as a guide to local celebrations:

> News that hostilities had ceased in Europe will be broadcast by the Prime Minister. It is expected that all churches will be open for thanksgiving and private prayer and that church bells will be rung.

A day or two later, the prime minister, Winston Churchill, broadcast to an expectant population that Germany had unconditionally surrendered and at midnight on 8 May hostilities in Europe would officially end. Within an hour of the prime minister's declaration, the victory bells of churches throughout Sussex were ringing in town and country and celebrations commenced immediately. The end of the war in Europe had come.

At Shoreham, the bells of St Mary's Church broke out into a grand peal of rejoicing as the prime minister broadcast the official news and bugles sounded the 'cease fire'.

Cease Fire Day became a public holiday, with post offices shutting within the hour leaving a reduced staff to man telephone exchanges and handle telegraph traffic. The following day also became a public holiday.

Throughout Sussex, flags and bunting appeared and there were very few buildings that did not display decorations. Street parties were held all over the county. Neighbours pooled their resources to provide a spread for children to enjoy. Jellies were made by melting down sweets and blancmanges with egg powder, coloured and flavoured. Children's parties were often combined with sports, cricket matches, fêtes and dancing in the streets until late in the evening, music sometimes provided by pianos dragged from houses for the purpose:

Loyal and patriotic Burgess Hill always has a procession on the occasion of National event. This was no exception; after an open air service and march past there were childrens sports an evening dance and entertainment, all held in the park. *(SX EXP)*

The following Sunday was observed as a special day of thanksgiving, with representative parades of units of all services and youth organisations taking place:

In victory parades and thanksgiving services Sussex people on Sunday joined hands and hearts with the nation at home and abroad. It was an historic occasion and associated with never forgotten scenes. In processions marched men, women, boys and girls, who had served the community during its years of stress and peril. In the religious services held in town parks and on village greens, members of all churches and those belonging to no denomination came together with one accord to acknowledge divine guidance in their great deliverance from evil and danger.

Many Sussex communities have already started preparation for the glad time "when the boys come home" and when they do return there will be celebration of the real end of the war, which can only be realised when the families are reunited.

For those who will never return Sunday's services naturally caused sad and tender thoughts. They will never be forgotten, nor the debt of the living to those who gave their all.

Wars may be won or lost, but they all leave a sense of national and personal disaster. *(SX EXP)*

At Hastings a parade and service was held at the Doodlebugged seafront church:

After meeting in a nearby hall, the congregation, led by a band and singing songs of praise made their way to the ruins of the old Church for a service and feast with entertainment. Then they held a two minutes silence at 11 40pm, the exact time the Church had been bombed. *(HC&STL OBS)*

The war in the Far East against Japan was, however, still raging, with many Sussex men still fighting. The news received on 15 August that Japan had capitulated bought much relief that the Japanese mainland was not to be invaded, as the loss of life was anticipated to be horrendous. Initial celebrations were somewhat muted compared to VE Day as reported in the *Sussex Express:*

TWO DAYS REJOICING, SUSSEX RECEIVES THE GREAT NEWS IN SPIRIT OF QUIET THANKFULNESS

Few had expected complete victory over Japan to be reached in three months after VE Day and the thankfulness of all was the greater on account of this great achievement. Wednesday was a quiet day throughout Sussex, except in a few of the more populous areas, with little public activity apart from official local announcements of victory, with dances and bonfires in the evening, but everywhere there was a less boisterous celebration than on VE Day.

CHAPTER 15

Peace returns

The rehabilitating of the South Downs after the tremendous impact of war was a serious problem. Many roads had been laid, a goodly number concreted and double tracked. The War Department's view that these new roads and the made-up old tracks would allow more motorists to visit the Downs was firmly rejected by the Society of Sussex Downsmen, who referred to them as 'a blot' on the landscape. At Seaford Head, for instance, there was a double concrete road in a figure of eight that had been constructed to carry heavy tank traffic. Concern was also voiced regarding the Cuckmere Valley and the surrounding downland between East Dean and Seaford.

As peace unfolded, the wartime achievements of many civilians became public, for instance: Mr and Mrs Kemp who lived in Lewes had looked after twenty-one evacuees throughout the war and 'only had fourteen' when the war ended. All the children came from London and had been looked after 'with the greatest kindness'. They all attended church, had post office savings accounts, where they saved their pocket money. As well as the children to look after every afternoon, Mrs Kemp attended the local YMCA (Young Men's Christian Association) and made the beds for around thirty soldiers. In June 1945, Mrs Kemp was selected to attend the civil defence stand-down parade in London as recognition for her work.

There were emotional scenes at Lewes Railway Station in July as about forty evacuees assembled to make the journey back to London for good. The youngsters looked fit and well and had obviously been well cared for. Some of the children spoke to the press and told them that they would miss the Sussex countryside and the Malling fields:

Tears were in the children's eyes as they said goodbye to their "aunties" and it was evident that several of the grownups present also had lumps in their throats as the little travellers went, waving fond "goodbyes" from the carriage windows. Another little drama of the war was over.

First class cricket resumed when Sussex played Northamptonshire in a one-day match at the Hastings Central Ground. Both teams fielded players who were still serving in the forces. Cricket lovers were only too pleased to pay out

1s (5p) admission to see a Sussex victory. Having declared at 244 for 4, Sussex bowled Northants out for just 77.

The first August bank holiday was celebrated in style. The *Sussex Express and County Herald* summed it up as 'Great and Glorious':

> Every place in Sussex, big and little, famous and obscure, inland and coast; shared in the joyful adventure of the greatest August Bank Holiday of all times.
>
> The County's seaside resorts, already overcrowded, found room for more. Some people moved out and made room for others to move in. How they managed it is a mystery, but even the bomb damaged and otherwise disturbed towns still suffering from a shortage of accommodation, reported the greatest holiday invasion ever experienced. People seemed willing to risk food and shelter to renew their acquaintance with the sea and introduce the youngest children to beach and sand for the first time. Many shared their bedrooms, even their beds, with strangers in preference to spending a night under the stars. Inconveniences and positive discomforts were gradually endured in the universal quest. There never was such a week-end or day out at the seaside.
>
> Smaller towns and villages celebrated the first August Bank Holiday of the restoration by reviving the local flower show, gymkhana or cricket match.
>
> Old familiar scenes on the main roads to the coast were re-enacted. The procession of cars started on Saturday and continued as a perpetual stream on Sunday and Monday and all day long the old inhabitants of places en route and others not so old, were entranced by the traffic pageant in which motor coaches made their reappearance.
>
> To complete the enjoyment of an unprecedented holiday, the sun gave warmth and brightness to the changing scene, until Monday afternoon when the summer weather exhausted its efforts and sought variety and relief in a few thunderstorms.
>
> But it was a great and glorious August Bank Holiday, a rich and well deserved reward for years of going without. *(SX EXP)*

The war was over, holidaymakers were returning, and the men were coming home. Sussex was getting back to normal.

Index